WHAT THE WORLD NEEDS NOW – HEALING MESSAGES FROM ANGELS

BY PAUL D WILLIAMS

Printed in Victoria, Canada

National Library of Canada Cataloguing in Publication Data

Williams, Paul D., 1963-
What the world needs now : healing messages from angels /
Paul D. Williams.
ISBN 1-4120-0415-2
1. Spirit writings.   I. Title.
BF1290.W54 2003   133.9'3   C2003-902944-1

TRAFFORD

This book was published *on-demand* in cooperation with Trafford Publishing.
On-demand publishing is a unique process and service of making a book available for retail sale to the public taking advantage of on-demand manufacturing and Internet marketing.
On-demand publishing includes promotions, retail sales, manufacturing, order fulfilment, accounting and collecting royalties on behalf of the author.

Suite 6E, 2333 Government St., Victoria, B.C. V8T 4P4, CANADA

Phone	250-383-6864	Toll-free	1-888-232-4444 (Canada & US)
Fax	250-383-6804	E-mail	sales@trafford.com
Web site	www.trafford.com	TRAFFORD PUBLISHING IS A DIVISION OF TRAFFORD HOLDINGS LTD.	
Trafford Catalogue #03-0784		www.trafford.com/robots/03-0784.html	

10   9   8   7   6   5   4   3   2

CONTENTS PAGE

CONTENTS CONTINUED.

*DENOTES POEMS.

THIS BOOK IS DEDICATED TO MY
BROTHER RICHARD AND MY
NEPHEW NEIL, WHO HAVE LEFT
THIS PHYSICAL REALM.
THERE IS NO SEPARATION.

MY THANKS TO NOEL, PIARAS, MY
SISTER GERALDINE AND ALSO MY
FRIENDS VERONICA AND ASHLING
FOR THEIR HELP.

CHAPTER ONE

My first client in healing was my then and present partner, Noel, (God bless him). I had watched his condition deteriorate over a period of four to five years. He had days, even weeks of immobility with a great deal of pain and discomfort, despite the fact that he was taking up to twenty-six assorted tablets per day. He had been diagnosed with osteoarthritis in his neck with an obstruction in the thoracic outlet. He was told this was an ongoing and degenerative condition. Pain management and long waiting lists were all he could be offered. He also had lumps on his wrists and fingers and also stiffness in his ankles. At this stage Noel was thirty-eight years old.

Something deep inside me knew that I could help, even heal Noel. Helping Noel to sleep was my first aim. Painkillers and muscle and nerve relaxants did not work when the pain was intense. I would place my hand on his head (what I now know to be his brow chakra) and found that if I synchronised my breathing with his, I was able to draw his attention away from his own breathing. He would often go into a deep sleep in minutes.

Another time I was sitting beside him and I could sense that he was in pain. Suddenly, I could see, through a vision or picture that flashed into my head, a red ball of energy in his arm. I asked if the pain was centred in that spot and he said yes, it was. I had the urge (or inspiration) to somehow take hold of the red ball of energy. I didn't know how to do this but I knew I could. It felt like I knew how to do this already, like a memory of an experience returning. I just used my imagination and imagined I could take the ball out, and I did. It worked. Noel could feel the pain moving out of his arm and into my hand. I did not feel the pain but felt the energy.

That night something happened to me. I felt a great sense of peace and love. I also became consciously and physically aware of something that I feel I have really always known but was afraid to say, think, or acknowledge. I was a healer. It is similar to knowing you are gay and scared of being who you really are. I was scared to acknowledge to myself that even I could be a healer. My mind would tell me that I was being silly. " Who do I think I am – Jesus?" My ego would shrink at the thought of hearing the words "I am a healer". The little "I" would laugh at me. "Who and what do you think you are now Williams? Don't even try it, don't think it and don't say it; you'll be laughed at, called a 'nut-case' – nuttier then you already are".

My attention was then drawn to my tarot cards that were left on a shelf. Again something told me "it is time".   I had the cards for about ten years, with the intention of studying them one at a time so I would learn them. I had already done some readings using the booklet that came with the pack. I would look up the cards in the book, get drawn to one or two words and a story seemed to develop

6

in my head. I didn't take this very seriously, even though the readings were accurate. Eventually the cards ended up on the shelf again. I never did study them.

Events started to change around this time for Noel and me. The handcraft business we had built up was becoming a strain and a burden. Noel could do less and less work. Even though he had a lot of pain he would force himself to work. Continuous chasing of orders to pay bills forced us both into a pattern of exhaustive bursts of activity to periods of long waiting for payment. Our cash flow wasn't flowing and the bills were mounting. It was taking too high a toll on our physical and mental health. We both knew it was time to stop.

Around the same time, something very strange and out of the ordinary occurred. I found myself in a bookshop. I had little interest in books. Actually I had no interest in books. At the age of about thirteen or fourteen a priest threw a Bible at me, hitting me on the head. I had asked the priest "who wrote the Bible and is it a true story"? The priest replied "it's not exactly a true story and was written by very clever people in such a way that not-so-clever people could understand what Jesus said". "So it's not true!" I replied. "It's a pack of lies!". His response was a flying book and he sent me home from school. As I left the school grounds, I crossed the road to the church on the corner. As I passed through the church grounds, I stopped and turned towards the school. I gave a two-finger salute and said aloud "I don't need you. I'll show you I don't need your pieces of paper". I turned to the church and gave the same salute. "Fuck you too. I'll find my own way to God!". I was angry. Any respect that I may have had for authority left me that day along with any respect I may have had for books and those who were book-learned. My rebellious teens had well and truly started. Anyway, twenty years later I found myself standing inside a bookshop that I would usually stand outside of, waiting for Noel. I walked to the section on spirituality and was immediately drawn to a particular book. It seemed to be shining in some way. It looked brighter then the others. It was as if the book said to me "come over and pick me up!" So I did. The book was about hands-on healing. I thumbed through a few pages with no particular interest. It looked very complicated to me. I looked at the price on the back of the book and quickly put it back on the shelf and left to wait outside for Noel. My ego was there again, horrified with me. "Thinking of giving in are you? Buying a book, conforming, spending over £20 on a book. You're stupid. You won't understand it. You won't be able to remember all that information. It's a big book". I went home without the book that day but I could not get it out of my mind. I knew I had to have it. Within a week or so I made the trip to town for no other reason than to buy the book. This may seem quite trivial to some, but for me it was a major shift in my way of thinking and acting.

I continued with my healing on Noel, mostly at night or when he was asleep. I took to my new book with gusto. Again something strange happened. I just read over the words, not trying to learn or retain any of the content. It was like I was scanning the information and would retrieve it when I needed it. Anyway, it was all above my head. I don't need to know how a thing or process works in order to use it. I did get invaluable information and energy from that book after reading it. I had a bit more confidence. I also knew that I was remembering rather than learning. Certain sections of the book would almost light up as I was reading. These sections were related to what was happening to Noel. Noel used to get himself into all sorts of positions and postures in order to get some relief from the pain. He sometimes knelt with his body parallel with the bed and with his head tilted to the side, resting on the bed. Sometimes he would keep this position for days. To top it all off, one day I stood at the end of his bed and said to him "do you know that you are responsible for your own pain? You believe you have arthritis. Your mother has it so you have to have it. It identifies you with your mother. You are holding on to it yourself". Well, if looks could kill! He didn't say a word, but still I heard him say " You bastard – you of all people. How can you possibly say that I am doing this, putting myself through this hell". We looked at each other for a few minutes without speaking. I left the room. Noel was seething and I was gob-smacked. Where did all that come from and why did I feel like I had spoken the truth? I wasn't going to apologise. I knew that my words had hurt Noel but they had hit home. In a way, it had hurt me a little to say them, but I got the courage from somewhere. I thank God. The god inside and outside of me because it started Noel on a journey of self-healing and myself on a journey of spiritual awareness.

We had set a date to close our business. I knew I could turn to the Tarot. Somehow it felt right. I had previously

9

torn out an advert from one of the newspapers looking for psychics for a Tarot line. I had it tucked away for months. I knew that I would use it someday. I made the call, and inquired if they knew of anybody who taught the Tarot. The man who runs the line gave me the number of an alternative healing centre in Dublin. When I made contact with the healing centre, they gave me four names and phone numbers. I rang and got through to three answering machines and one live speaker, named David. He was starting a six-week course on the Tarot the next evening and there was a place available. I could not have planned it better, but there was no plan, on my part anyway. Or so I thought.

CHAPTER TWO

I was feeling a mixture of being nervous, excited, and relaxed as I walked up the short narrow staircase in the healing centre. It led to four empty rooms, a washroom and the tiny reception area in what seemed to be a former cupboard or closet. I had the sense that this was the start of something – like the first moments of a roller-coaster ride. "What am I getting myself into?" I was also on my guard. The ego was there, making sure I wasn't conforming, walking into some sort of crazy cult. I was firm with myself. No group cuddles or hugs, no religious stuff and no bonding with any group or any individual in it. This was also something new for the relationship between Noel and myself. Ever since a couple of weeks after we first met, we were inseparable, living and then working together. We had moved from Dublin to a cottage in the country. We stopped drinking (alcohol) together, so there was not a lot of socialising. We spent almost ten years in constant companionship and it now seemed like this was some kind of parting, the end of that consistency.
We went for a walk the previous evening to talk about where this new direction would lead us. At that time I saw it as a natural progression for me. It felt right that I should be doing this now. I also knew that I would be working from home on a Tarot line! This was a means to an end, an income, but I also knew in my gut, my inner-knowing, that this was somehow connected with the healing energy I

had discovered. Noel was a bit apprehensive. He had concerns about the "occult" label often attached to the Tarot cards and the "cult" label often attached to spiritual groups. He was also apprehensive of spirit contact. He was observing distinct changes in me. I was becoming a different person to the one he had been living with all these years. I was talking about auras and energies. I was reading a book, writing poetry and now a group! We both felt a little threatened. I agreed to take things slowly, see how it developed – and we would check in with each other as it unfolded.

I was surprised to see that David was younger then me. He had a pleasant and friendly personality. I liked him straight away, although I was still defensive and was doing my own reading on him, as I knew he was doing on me. The first thing David told the group of seven or eight people was to respect the integrity of the group and that whatever went on within the group was to stay within the group. With this in mind I will uphold that integrity.

Within six weeks I was doing Tarot readings. It came naturally to me. Within ten weeks I was working on a well-known Tarot line from my bedroom. Needless to say, David was and is a very good teacher. I went on to do a further six-week course with David, a spiritual awareness course. It covered spirit guides, spiritual healing, the auras, chakras and crystals, as well as direct contact with the spirit world. Again, with respect to the circle of people I sat with, I leave these wonderful experiences within the circle.

During the course of my time with David, he had on two occasions introduced us to a man called Vinnie, a very wise and magical man. During a talk, Vinnie used one particular word, a word that struck a cord in me. It was like I needed to be told this in order for it to be reactivated in my mind. That word is "magic". Vinnie had said "you are magic". It was like my mind burst open, expanded. A flood of memories and flashes of images came into my head. I had always seen it. I knew of this magic; the flowers, the grass, the trees, the constant changing colours around me – the sky, the stars, the sun; life in all its assorted shapes and forms. I had always seen this magic, and labelled it as a boy with the word "magic". I had a feeling that I recognised, only this time it was stronger. (It gets stronger each time I experience it which is almost constantly at this stage of my life). It is impossible to describe a feeling. Like a taste, you have to experience it for yourself to know it and then you will only know it your way.

The first time I felt this way was in a dream state (asleep), not long after Noel and I met and not long after my brother Richard had passed over into spirit (or died). I became aware of Richard's presence. I had experienced this at his bedside just before he passed over. Now, it felt like he was holding my hand or we were somehow attached to each other. I could not feel my body and was aware that I could not move it. It was like I was pinned or weighed down on the bed. It was a pleasant, warm feeling and I was not scared. I felt at peace. I then had a sensation of movement, a rushing upward at a fantastic speed and a terrific sense of freedom and space. I imagine it would be similar to a combination of sky and sea diving. The movement got faster and faster. I could sense laughter and happiness or joy. It was dark at first with a strange yellow/red glow that seemed to be around me. Maybe it *was* me. We then passed through what seemed to be layers of clouds of colour, a foggy transparent surreal world or worlds. Then we burst into a bright golden-yellow light and I could sense and see millions of small balls of light. They were completely surrounding me. Balls or beings of happiness, energising each other with this overwhelming happiness. I can only describe it as being like a bubble in a fizzy drink, surrounded by other bubbles, but with a sense of feeling. I knew that these beings only had to merge or pass through each other to share an experience much more intense than any that could be shared between people. Even better than the best sexual experience of people merging with each other. There was a sense of oneness. One thought was thought by all. They were or seemed curious. I could see all the colours that I knew, in each one. One of them came up to my face and a face and bust of a woman pushed out, as though through a membrane or thin rubber wall, like a balloon. She smiled, merged back in a ball of colour and whisked away. All through this I still had the sensation of movement and the connection to Richard. He was showing me and letting me feel where he was. It was getting brighter and brighter. We were moving into a huge ball of white light. Light brighter than the sun but similar. I remember I opened my eyes in reality (or this reality). I found myself sitting up in bed. I could still feel the connection and sensation of moving into the light. I

14

looked at Noel and closed my eyes again. "Richard, I am not ready to go into the Light", I said or thought. " I have a new life starting". Something was telling me "No, not yet". I sensed Richard knew this and was only showing me all this because he could. I don't know or need to know why this happened. I do know that it did. Just after I said I was not ready, I found myself back in my body, as such. Back, still sitting up in bed. Noel was asleep, oblivious to what had gone on.

This experience was more intense than when I had experienced Richard's spirit touch or pass through me as he passed over. That time I felt a tremendous sense of peace. Everything was OK. I was touched by the essence of love. As were the rest of my family at that time. We floated out of the hospital when we said goodbye to Richard. That energy seemed to carry us over the whole period of his funeral. I know now that this energy is around all comings and goings, births and deaths but sometimes our own pain can block us off from it.

It was only after this second experience of Richard's spirit that I become aware of the fact that this feeling was familiar to me. I had experienced the same sensations when, after having consumed a lot of alcohol, my father and I found ourselves in the River Liffey in Dublin. I could not keep myself above the water no matter how hard I tried and then I stopped trying. It was all right. I felt good. The cold had gone. I was at peace and there was a white light that I was curious about. I had the most pleasant feeling of safety. Next thing I knew, I was against the wall with nothing to hold on to. I was going under again. I didn't resist. That was OK. A hand then grabbed me by the scruff of the neck. I was back at the wall again. Nothing to hold on to again; and under again. I just wanted to go. Again, a hand pulled me up and then a life ring was thrown and hit me on the head. I was still very drunk. My father seemed to have sobered up with the shock. As I looked up from the river I could see a Garda (Irish policeman) at the wall together with a whole crowd of people watching. And me, in my rebellion against authority (I was only sixteen at this time), started shouting at the Garda that he had tried to kill me and had tried to drown me, hitting me with the life belt.

Anyway, I was hauled out and despite fire engine, ambulance and police cars being present, we had to walk home, mainly because of my abuse. Also, when the Garda heard that we were going to a high crime and impoverished area of Dublin, he told us to walk. My prejudices met his! Just to conclude this story, the night was still young (actually, early morning). We had been at a wedding party. When we returned to the groom's house and the earlier events were told, all the focus went to my mother! My poor mother, she could have lost her husband and son. I was given whiskey to warm me up. It didn't, it riled me up further. I was boiling. I had nearly drowned and my mother was getting the attention and sympathy and my father, well, that was another matter. I don't know what possessed him in the first place to pick me up and hold me over his head. "You! You bastard! You tried to kill me. You just picked me up and threw me into the river. But you didn't let go in time". He made a lunge at me and all Hell broke loose. I stormed out wearing only a shirt and baggy trousers belonging to my granddad. Bare-footed, that night I slept in a car and shivered the morning hours in. I went from Heaven to Hell in a few short hours. I have to acknowledge now that no matter how I got into the river, my dad did save my life.

Richard came to me a third time, all within a year of his passing. On this occasion it was just before the first anniversary. I had decided to put a gift on his grave, one of the crafts that we had made. I think putting the craft on his grave was more to do with marketing than mourning. As I was putting the finishing touches to the gift, I sensed a very warm heat beside me and a glow, a sense of happiness. I recognised it as Richard and a huge smile broke out. Noel was in the room at the time. I went into a trance. I remember feeling like a statue. I couldn't move a muscle and I could sense, almost see but not quite, a very bright warm ball over my head. I felt myself sitting back in the chair and he spoke to me in my head. He told me he would not be back for a while, gave me a message for my mother, and left. Noel was watching this. He said the whole corner of the room lit up with a golden light and so did my face. He saw me looking up in awe at something, smiling, laughing, talking and nodding. He also said how he felt the warmth and the peaceful feeling.

So I was by no means closed to the idea of spirit or the spirit world, but I still, as yet, regarded it as something in the future, after the death of the body. I had the same notion about any god. I believed in a source of energy, something in charge of the magic, yet apart and separate from it, that we or I would be reunited with in another life or after-life. Have I changed my mind? Yes, big time!

CHAPTER THREE

My interest in healing was growing. I could also see from my own life-path all the stages and changes I had made were now leading to somewhere or something. It all started to make sense to me. As if I had just been given the missing part of a puzzle, a part missing that allowed the other pieces to fit into place. I asked around about Reiki healing after I had seen a flyer in a health shop window (I was passing by, not a customer). I went along to an open workshop one evening. While I did feel relaxed with the energy and I could feel it flowing through me, I was not fully relaxed in the all-female group. This was unusual for me. Later on I had the Reiki One initiation with another Reiki master, who had been introduced to me through David's group.

Over a three-month period I learned breathing techniques and visualisations to connect to spirit and healing energies, to focus my intention and trust what I was sensing, feeling, hearing, seeing or visualising. I was not relying on anybody to tell me yes or no, right or wrong, just myself to trust my own intuition and senses. Not a very long time three months, yet I had experienced and became aware of more that I had in the previous thirty years. I was becoming spiritually aware and it was becoming second nature to me.

Because I was working on the Tarot line I found myself open or channelling for twelve hours a day, five days a week. I was also working daily on myself, working on my own energy field or aura with crystals and stones. Some of the pauses in-between readings became meditations. I was still experiencing changes to my personality. I felt a lot calmer in myself and with those around me. Although I was always very close to, and aware of the magic of nature, I felt I was getting even closer becoming more a part of it. Every day was amazing.

During the readings, I was experiencing flashbacks of other peoples' memories, issues from their childhood that had become part of their adult lives. I was also able to pinpoint what they needed to do in order to deal with these issues. I also noticed that a lot of the time I was not reading the cards but looking out of the window and just talking. I was starting to tune into other peoples' feelings, including pain and discomfort (although I would only feel it briefly). Sometimes their pain would go during the reading. My readings were taking on a very spiritual and also very healing nature. The clients on the other end of the phone could feel the energy around them changing. Their loved ones in spirit would touch them. They could feel a breeze or a tingle, a heat or a chill and then a smile and even if only for a moment or two, a sense of peace. This did not happen with all the readings at first. Some clients were looking for fortune telling and I found that that was not what I was doing. Those callers did not stay very long with me. A lot of callers were quite psychic themselves and had some spiritual experiences, seen or heard spirits or knew when something was about to happen. I found it to be quite a taboo subject. A lot of people did not talk or tell anyone about their experience for fear of being labelled crazy, even though most were already labelled crazy or the odd one out of their family.

When I started readings on the phone line I had to use a pseudonym. This was a clause in a yearlong contract that I signed. This in itself was a huge thing for me to do (more changes). I was using a speakerphone. The only room I had to work in was the bedroom where Noel spent most of his time. He was a silent witness to a lot of these events. He never did get as amazed as I did with what was happening but I could see that it was having some effect. He could not deny his own ears and was losing his fear or apprehension of the spirit world. He was also at a point of desperation where his pain was concerned. He could see the changes taking place in me. That, along with having witnessed the readings, opened him up to the possibility that there might be something in this and besides he had nothing to loose except some pride maybe. So Noel started using the crystals and stones and I continued to do healing with him, more focused.

Shortly after I finished with David I went on to do a further course that was called "Journey Into Spirit" with a lady called Mary. While David did not get into angels and saints, Mary was a different story. My first impression was all angelic and light (until I got to know her a bit better). She is very down to earth. She is a lovely and very special person. At this stage I had a very clear connection to my guides who were changing every six or eight weeks. I was becoming aware of different spirit energy around me, just as I was aware of different people around me.

On my first night with Mary's group she gave me a copy of "The Great Invocation" along with some information on St. Germane. I still connected angels and so called saints with the Catholic Church, and my mind was closed until now. Mary introduced me to the pendulum, automatic writing and to archangel retreats (which she came across in a book by a well-known angel teacher).

She also introduced me to the book. As I was reading the book, again it felt like I was remembering and not learning. I knew all this stuff already at a deeper level. It was like a dormant volcano of information. On one level, this was not all that strange as I had always been getting answers and solutions to questions and problems, seemingly from nowhere. I had learned to trust this to some degree. Things used to sort themselves out, or I'd be in the right place at the right time. When I look back over my life so far, it seems as though I have always been guided into situations and from one situation to another. Mary taught me about the Violet Flame of St Germane and "The Great Invocation" that mentioned God and Christ and the Holy Spirit; my first brush with that so-called "holy" stuff. Unusually, I didn't react, I didn't put up my old defences and blocks. I went along with the flow, let it happen and Wow – did it happen!

I started to get teachings, talks, lectures and information from Spirit both day and night, also during and in-between readings. When I was sleeping I no longer went into a mishmash of events, I went to visit the different realms of the spirit world; all those coloured levels of cloud-like substance that I had passed through with Richard's spirit.

There were temples and gardens, mountains, lakes and seas. I met and talked with translucent beings dressed in robes. I also met with beings of pure love and light, some too bright to look at so that I could only wallow in their presence. There was one place in the spirit world (if I could call it a place), that had a profound effect on me. I followed an exercise in the book to visit a highly evolved spirit who made himself known to the author. On my first journey or visit, I visualised the steps and the door opening and then I heard a voice say "this door will always be open to you, Paul". I walked into what looked like a Roman or Greek bathhouse. I saw pillars of what seemed like marble, around a sunken floor or pool with a mosaic of an eagle in the centre. To the left, in the corner, was a small table with a candle and a bowl of water. I went over and lit another candle. I just thought, "candle" and had one in my hand. When I turned there was a man standing there. A tall, slender figure who had a golden glow around him. He looked Oriental. He was dressed in a long brown gown-type garment that had a granddad shirt type collar. He looked young, in his mid to late twenties. I thought maybe a monk or a priest of some sort. We sat on the steps leading to the sunken mosaic floor and talked. I cannot remember the conversation. I know that he seemed vaguely familiar like I knew him before now. I do remember him telling me that I had work to do. I have had many of these experiences with these vague, familiar memories but I cannot remember the conversations and teachings.

Then things took a different twist. During my readings, I started to connect to the energy of so-called saints and I would recognise their presence. I would ask the caller "are you or your mother, father or anyone praying to or petitioning a saint?" I was naming saints that I had never even heard of. While all the details of those readings are confidential, I will give an example of one of the first of these saintly visits. I answered the phone as usual. The woman at the other end was sobbing. Within seconds I could feel her deep depression. She was in a dark place. I started her reading as normal and went back into her past to where the pain had started. I was then aware of a presence; a man, a monk. I could see him in my minds' eye. I got a name, "Saint Martin". "Do you pray to St. Martin?" I asked. She stopped sobbing. I could feel the realisation hitting her, giving her strength. She said "I have never made a phone call to anything like this before. I have never had a Tarot reading. But a few minutes ago I was feeling very low and I threw myself onto my bed sobbing. I asked out loud for Saint Martin to help me. My hand went under the pillow and touched a piece of paper, crunched up in a ball. It distracted me and I opened it, tears running down my face. It was a shop receipt and on the back of it there were advertisements and special offers. Your phone number was there. Without thinking I dialled and got through to you". The energy then changed. I could feel her heart opening. A sense of peace overcame her. She had stopped crying. "Do you feel the peace?" I asked. "Yes" she replied. "Do you feel the love?" I asked. "Yes" she replied again. "Have you a smile on your face?" I asked. "Yes, yes" she laughed and I felt a surge of energy running through her. "I haven't felt like this in years" she said. "I've been in and out of hospital with all sorts of doctors and counsellors and psychiatrists. None of them worked for me. I feel so good". She cried again. I felt tears of rejoicing, and cried also.

A lot of my readings were similar to this, except that the energy or spirit that came through was that of a loved one, family member, or an unborn or very young child – which was OK with me. Even though I knew it was all extraordinary, they were just ordinary spirits to me. The latest development however, was different, or so I thought. Saints to me were elitist and anything that had an elitist energy or order to it was alien to me. Deep inside I had always felt some form of equality. The idea of one person being any more than another did not wash with me despite outward trappings of money, education or achievements, accents and position in life. I always thought that if you put people naked in a room for a while, they would soon know that there are no superior ones among them. I now had to bring this thought process about the physical level into another level, the spiritual level. For me, the perceived separation between the two was dissolving. Besides, the energy I felt with St. Martin was by no means elitist, it was so open and loving and honest.

It was around this time that I started to write or channel information. Mary had suggested that we keep a diary of our experiences, but I never did. I was in contact with my guides constantly. Some of their names were getting very biblical for my liking. Isaac and Isaiah came and left. Then came Elijah with Benjamin and Bartholomew. These three stayed with me the longest so far. They have moved on now.

CHAPTER FOUR

I tried to use the pendulum, asking my guides for "yes" or "no" answers. This will usually work for anybody but my guides were having none of it. They would just say to me "listen and trust". The trust was about myself. They were telling me not to be asking them to make my decisions for me or foretell future events but trust my own decision process and allow the future to unfold as it will. This was the best way they could help me. My guides had the same attitude towards the automatic writing. I would close my eyes and hold the pen on the paper. I would start moving it across the page only to find a message asking me why I wouldn't just listen and write what I heard, trusting what was coming through to me. So that is what I did, and still do.

Then one day I started to receive the following messages. They were not just for me, or for anyone in particular, but for a wider audience. Well, that's OK for someone looking for fame and fortune but I was quite comfortable working under an alias, hidden away in my bedroom, even though at a deeper level I had always thought that one day I would write my own book. This was another reason I gave myself not to read books – my mind would not be a mixture of everybody else's concepts! Warped thinking on my part, I know. It was as though I thought that by keeping my mind "clear" of the ideas of others I would be able to access my very own alphabet and hitherto unused words. Psychic people had also told me on a number of occasions that I would write a book. I was told "your words will reach the common man". I had also been given my own pointers during meditation and visualisations into other realms where I received a quill, a golden pen and a blue ball of light which was put in my throat by a guide. All these are symbols of communication and boy, was I communicating! And in a way that I never, in my wildest dreams or ego-trips, could have imagined. The shear joy and sense of helping I got produced in me a deep satisfying glow and warmth with each reading or healing. It was then, and still is, like food for my soul.

It was about January 2000 that the messages started to come. I really did not know what to do with them so I collected them in a drawer. I had also started to paint and write poetry before I started the spiritual work. Up to this point my poems were mostly angry and my paintings the same. This took a sudden shift. I was writing and painting in-between calls and so I was constantly open to healing energy which started to emerge through all aspects of my work. I became very sensitive to feeling energy at this stage. I could feel the energy flowing from the paintings. I could also feel it flowing into them. The paintings, in turn, were cleansing the energy around them. As I was writing some of the poems I could feel the words touching my heart and I knew the energy would touch some of those who read or heard the poems.

I was suddenly hit by the realisation of how real all this was. Sometimes it was a lonely place to be. Most people don't want to know about this "stuff" (or so I thought). It was with this thought in mind that the penny dropped. I realised I was scared. My fear was showing itself to me.

There was an inner struggle going on. In many ways my life was detached from mainstream society. I didn't socialise, attend sporting or religious gatherings. I was not particularly involved with family issues any longer – or at least these issues did not affect me as they used to. I was doing OK minding my own business and now I found myself worrying how everyone or most people would think of me, label or judge me. I had been here before when I was facing the realisation of my sexuality twelve years ago. I was gay, married and had a four-year-old son. That fear had brought me to the edge of despair and the point of suicide. Again it was something deep inside that told me I was worth loving and stopped me going over the edge. I made major changes in my life and told whomever I needed to tell. I stopped pretending and allowed me to be me. Within a few weeks I had met Noel. Noel has always had a calming effect on me. He taught me self-respect, which I did not have when I met him. He stopped me getting carried away with myself and looking for quick-fix solutions to any issues I found myself involved in. He has been my greatest (if this is an appropriate word) teacher and I truly believe that without him I would be in a very dark place. My lack of self-respect would have led me onto a different path. I am aware that my path is and was my choice but, credit where credit is due, he played a vital part in the way I made my choices.

It now seemed that the tables were turned. Addicted to painkillers and tranquillisers that were not working, Noel was depressed and in a very dark place. He is a very independent minded person with his own views on life (as we all have). I knew I had to handle this very carefully and sensitively. I started talking about his childhood, listening for key words. I knew nothing of, nor had I ever had any training in, counselling, but I found myself using what seemed to my mind counselling techniques. As he was talking, certain words would stand out or light up in my head. I would use these words back to him, usually with a question. It was like we were going into different rooms, with each key word leading to another room. We were looking at where Noel had built his thought process; the different stages of his personality development. We looked to see who gave this or that belief or trait to his personality. We looked at the boundaries within which his mind was working and at what he would or would not allow himself to think, feel or do. We were looking at his very strong connection to his mother (who had and still has arthritis). We looked at how this was having an effect on his life today. These talks went on over a period of about three months, often with breaks of weeks in between. I was also doing work on his chakras. Again, I had no training in this field. I found myself doing it instinctively. I told him his root or base chakra was closed and he needed to connect to the Earth more, to do some gardening and walking. To my surprise, he did as he was advised! Noel was on the mend. He loved gardening and the birds and all of nature. I would watch him from the bedroom window as I worked. I could see him coming back to life, as such, in front of my eyes, although he still has his limits. He was also told to dance and while I have no problem dancing around the house, I have never seen Noel dance. Maybe he dances inside, who knows? Within six months and for the first time in seven years, Noel had no pain in his neck. The raw nerve sensation had gone from his shoulders and arms. The morning stiffness in his wrists and ankles was gone, as were the lumps that were developing on his wrists and fingers. Noel had let go of his arthritis and now found a tablet addiction to overcome; another battle which he faced with great courage and dignity, although on a number of occasions he just stopped the lot, went cold turkey and into depression. These were stepping-stones on his road to recovery.

Meanwhile, I was reading books like they were going out of fashion. As I was reading, I had a sense of "I know all this already" and a sense of support of some kind which reassured me that I wasn't alone or going out of my mind. One day, as I was lying with my chakra set on me, I was in a deep meditative state but fully conscious. I sensed guides around me. I felt and had a vision of them branding me with symbols on both my hands and into my heart. The cross, the Star of David and a crescent moon with a ball or globe beneath it. My body has felt lighter since this and seems to be getting lighter still. I don't feel as heavy as I used to. My guides told me that I had been given an initiation into healing energy and that I should move to

31

county Leitrim. I was told to open a healing centre and bring the light to Leitrim.

At this time Mary told me about a shamanic workshop she had attended. She was now organising groups to go to these workshops and invited me to join. "You'll love it" she said, "using drums and rattles and journeying and dancing". It sounded a bit off-the-wall to me but, Hey!, I was connecting to dead people almost every day. There did not seem to be any separation between "work" and "not work". I was quickly learning non-judgement. I wasn't too sure if this shamanic business was for me, so I decided to give it a try. We had just moved to Leitrim when I went to my first shamanic workshop and met a teacher named Martin. I had come home. Shamanism came naturally to me. I had been working for 9 months on the phone line and a lot of weird and wonderful things had happened. I had done over 1000 readings/healings by this time. I realised that what Martin was teaching and telling us was already happening to me. I just did not know what it was. The flashbacks I was seeing were soul retrievals. I sometimes saw and mentioned animals to some of my callers. These were in fact, power animals. The ancient wisdom that is called Shamanism is alive. Martin taught me how to use it in a more focused way, or rather allow it to use me by me focusing on it. This suited me because this went beyond religion, angels and saints, something I had known and said to many clients.

So here I was, getting quite comfortable with my life, when I was taken on another journey while attending another workshop. "Journeying" is what shamans do and have always done. They travel (through meditation) to the different spirit worlds to receive information and healing energy. Sometimes this is in the form of power animals and sometimes in the form of soul parts that have left, due to some trauma or shock. Shamans retrieve or bring back these soul parts to those who seek their help and assistance. On the journey in question, I was brought to the Upper World. I found myself in a familiar chamber. I was surprised as I had not intended or set out to go there. I found myself lying on a couch or plinth. A stream of spirits came, stood around me and touched me. It felt like an electrical charge was running through me and that I was floating an inch or two above the ground. It was overwhelming, as if every cell in my body was vibrating. There was a thunderstorm outside during this journey. When I came back into the room and into my body I was so overcome with emotion that I had to leave the room. As I opened the front door to go outside there was a bolt of lightening followed immediately by a crash of thunder. This was getting surreal, like a movie or dream, but I knew it was real. It took me a while to take it in and to digest all the information that had come to me. I had been touched by many ascended masters who, up until now, were still a bit elitist for me. There was nothing elitist about their energy. It was the energy of love, just pure unconditional love for all that there is. Again this felt familiar to me. I had felt this energy before, somewhere, sometime.

Just to round off the events of the weekend; as I drove home I stopped to watch a thunderstorm move across the sky. I phoned Noel. We were about sixty miles apart and there was no thunderstorm where Noel was. As we spoke I said " there is another flash of lightening" and Noel jumped. There was a brief disconnection for a second or two and Noel said "lightening has just struck the ground outside the window"!   I thought I was leaving the surreal world back in the workshop. I had to accept all this as real. I didn't really care about anyone else's opinion of me. I just had to get my own head around it. As for Noel, he could not deny all these strange things happening either. The best was yet to come.

CHAPTER FIVE

I was coming to terms with the new situation. The ascended masters were working with me. I wasn't a wet day at this, with the notion that the masters came at the end of a lifetime of or at least years of spiritual practice and meditation. Of course, this is nonsense. There is no elitism when it comes to spiritual energy. It is available to all that are open to it, without exception. Being open could simply mean picking up a book or, as I myself experienced it, picking up the phone.

I finished working on the line with almost 3000 readings done. I was still doing a course with Mary and then, one night, something happened that took Mary out of the group. I found myself "talking" or "holding" the energy of the group. I was also connecting with the individual members of the group in a way similar to the way I connected with clients on the phone. I was connecting to and could feel what was going on in their energy fields. This happened on a number of nights. Something would intervene so that Mary could not be there and I would lead the group. When Mary's course finished some of the group asked me to continue. I knew this was the way I was heading and so did Mary. On one occasion in a shamanic workshop, Mary announced to my surprise, "Paul is starting a course next week". The way and speed with which all this was happening did not give me much time to get scared or allow my fears and doubts to block me. I just did it and it worked.

One evening, Noel and I were driving to the nearby town of Manorhamilton. A few miles outside the town there is a small mountain or large hill. I have always been drawn to what looks like the symbol of a cross on one side. It had a magnetic attraction for me. This time, as I approached the mountain, I felt myself opening up or connecting with spirit. It was different this time. It came not in the usual way it had been coming for over a year but was a stronger, larger or brighter presence. It is hard to put words to feelings or energies. The energy felt male. Then this spirit introduced himself to me as Jason, my Guardian angel. His energy was beautiful, loving, graceful and humble. I could feel all this moving through me. I told Noel what was happening (as I do) and then, as we passed the mountain I had another look. I could see a mist, a bright mist on the side of the mountain. There was no mist anywhere else and it was not the time of day for the mist to rise from the fields. I told Noel to look as I was driving. The mist formed into two symbols - the Star of David and the Crescent Moon. I saw them quite clearly, briefly but clearly. As I had to watch the road, Noel continued to look. He confirmed that he saw the symbols too. This all occurred in the space of a minute or so and things like these were starting to become so normal that we just drove on. What else could we do? While Noel went about his business in Manorhamilton, I stayed in the van. Again, Jason came through. This time he gave me a message about the symbols and how I had agreed to bring a message to the world (and we were only going shopping!).

Now angels were entering into the picture – my picture. The changes that were happening within that picture were happening in the most strange and unexpected ways and at the most strange and unexpected times. Angels! What next? Nothing less than archangels and they want me to write and publish a book and open the Archangel Michael School of Healing.

But first I was to set up a web-site. I can just about make a call on my mobile phone, but if it's a web-site they want, that's what they'll get. My son, who was 16 at the time, had been living with us for 4 years. He is also a healer in the making and he can see auras quite clearly. He can see and sense spirit and also travels on shamanic journeys. Most appropriately he is computer literate so a web-site was designed and launched. I started sending the message and symbols to all sorts of people and organisations, religious and political, spiritual and cultural. Not surprisingly, few of them acknowledged or replied.

I never expected anything more (or dare I say higher) to happen. I didn't expect all that had happened so far. Then the ultimate happened, again in a workshop on a journey! I found myself moving toward the same light Richard had brought me to the edge of, almost twelve years ago. This time I went into the Light. This is hard to put into words. The feelings were ecstatic, peaceful and above all, joyful. I could sense a jolly old man full of love, like a child might see Santa Clause. Then, out of the brightness came an even brighter ball of light. In front of me were a golden throne, a huge emerald-green robe and a ball floating where a head would be. Just as quickly as they appeared, they vanished. In a deep echoing man's voice I heard the words "I know you don't like all this 'king' stuff ". He chuckled and said, "just kidding". I laughed too. I felt and knew that this is what I have called 'Source' or 'God'. Yet I know that this is only a taste of All-That-Is, that God is still something greater, and greater again. I realised this energy wasn't just male even though I said "old man". It was also a kind old lady. Both male and female rolled into one. And that is what you and I are too.

CHAPTER SIX

I hadn't asked anybody or spirit "what's an angel?". I don't
remember even thinking it. I was becoming more aware of
angels through the books I was reading, but only recently.
Although I was aware of Jason and angel energy, I was still
working with my guides. I was told or it was impressed
onto me that it was time to start writing. I had been
getting the messages from spirit over the past year or so.
They would come out of the blue. I never sat with the
intention of asking a question or expecting to receive a
message, they had been spontaneous. Now I was asked to
simply listen and write. So I took to my bed and after two
weeks I had the messages about angels, messages from
archangels Michael and Gabriel, messages about the inner-
child, cutting of the ties and baggage. I had already started
the web-site with most of the remainder of the messages
and information on healing posted on it. Most of the
poems just happened spontaneously over the past two
years. When I gathered all this material together, I realised
I had enough for a book. How ironic! I, who not very
long ago had no time for angels, spirituality or books, now
writing one about angels and spirituality. There are many
books published both simple and complicated, covering
some of the material in this book i.e. reincarnation, karma,
inner-child, spiritual awareness, angels and healing. All of
these subjects are fairly new to my mind and vocabulary,
yet my use of them goes beyond what I have recently read

or even written. It feels comfortable or right. I am at ease and I seem to have a deeper knowing, beyond understanding, like as if I planted a seed. I know it will grow into something but I don't necessarily understand why or how.

Not being academically minded, I can be quite absent-minded when it comes to facts and figures. Faces and places, yes, but names, dates and details like what time it is now, I don't seem to have a capacity or a need to retain. I can ask for or find the information I need when I need it so the details of how and when and in what order these messages came will remain irretrievable in the past. I never bothered to date them, although most of my poems are signed and dated.

I do know the first message was "message to human kind" and was passed to me by my guide called Elijah. I was both frightened and excited. I was excited with the speed and clarity of the communication but very frightened about its content, or rather its destination – the world. I showed it to a few people. One man said it was about me and the need in me to change the world. Another person, a lady, was interested in it. She said she would de-code it and get back to me. She never did. Yet another lady said in a matter-of-fact way, "that's for the book that you will write" and handed it back to me. That was about two years ago and the message remained hidden among unfinished poems.

The way I would normally receive information or communicate with guides was through intuition. I didn't know this at the time. Intuition is when information is passed to you like you know it already. There seems to be a feeling of confidence so that you can impart the information. It is sometimes like going out on a limb and trusting it is not going to snap under your weight. As with names or very private details, you learn the difference between what is yours and what is new and you pass on the new information, whatever it may be. The means by which you get this message across and the manner in which you present it is up to you. This is how it is with me for most of my healing readings but when the messages came they came in a more direct manner, word for word in my inner ear. I didn't hear sounds. It was an inner voice, but not my own. I was aware of my guides' energy. I could sense them and was very familiar with them and had built up a trust or relationship and the feeling of love and peace that came with them, left me in no doubt that their intentions were loving and peaceful. Yet the messages were from a different voice to that of Elijah. I would ask, "who is this?", only to receive the answer "trust your intuition. Do you feel comfortable with the energy?" They would tell me I do not need to know or sometimes they would say, "who would you like me to be? I can give you any name that will please you". This went on between us for a while and I would challenge them, asking them if they were from the Light and working for the highest and purist good of myself and the highest and purist good of all. Each time they would repeat the words saying "Yes, I am from the light", etc. I would challenge them three times. I could

41

sometimes see the colour gold in my mind's eye while they answered the challenge. The only reason I was challenging them was that I sensed a different energy or vibration to that of my guides; stronger, more serious or focused. Not authoritarian, but certain. It took me a while to allow them to connect with me and that was only after I checked it out first with Elijah. Then they told me the reason why I didn't get a name. I was working with an energy ray from the ascended masters from a level of full awareness.

I didn't know the contents of this book at that time, so it was all somewhat puzzling. I had read about ascended masters. These are what we or I would know as saints; Buddha, Mary, Jesus, Krishna, Mohammed and all who lived a spiritual life on earth and found enlightenment or awareness. Whether they came to prominence or not, they are highly evolved or holy and close to the angels and Source (or God). An energy ray is like a radio signal that you tune into. When you hear about faith healing, hands-on, Reiki, spiritual healing etc., all of these work with energy rays that most people cannot see. These rays connect with our auras. I now believe/know that it is these rays that allow life, as we perceive it, to exist. They are beyond our understanding but not our knowing or intuition. I now see that what I thought was magic is in fact the miracle.

The book will now take you on a journey towards self-healing and spiritual awareness. I have interspersed some poems throughout the book. These seem to shorten and simplify the messages. While I did write these messages, they are not my words so you may notice a change to the flow. I would recommend that you read the book in full before doing any of the exercises.

Peace be with you.

I AM
WORTHY
TO RECEIVE YOU,
I AM
HEALED.

CHAPTER SEVEN

Non-Judgmentalism

A very simple way to be non-judgmental is to take responsibility for yourself. This means being in control of your own feelings so that what you see or hear outside of you has no effect on you. If you can isolate your feelings from outside influences while still remaining part of what is outside of you, you can observe happenings without these happenings having an effect on you.

If you can see the whole of life as a film (remembering that you personally can ever only see a tiny part of a much larger picture, like as if you had tunnel vision), you are part of the making of this film. This is an epic with a cast of billions and unlimited budget. The set is called "Earth" and the film is titled "Time". The story line has so many twists and turns, scenes within scenes and so many directors, actors, producers and set- designers etc., that no one knows or has the mental capacity to understand the plot. Yet each one has their own part to play or job to do with no awareness of the details of anyone else's part or job – only awareness that all have a part. If you can simply accept your own path and allow others to play their part (whatever it may be) without comparing it to yours, you cannot now be judgmental of the scenes that are played out in your line of vision. <u>All is well.</u>

When you judge another's role as wrong or insignificant, badly acted or incompetent, or if you condemn, you are taking on the role of the writer – the creator of the film and with this comes the weight of the world on your shoulders. You will feel burdened and responsible for all of what you judge. When you are non-judgmental you hand this back to the creator and allow the film, "Time", set on Earth, to play itself out, as it will, with or without your interference. In your own part, comparing what you see to the limit of what you think you know (which is limited to what you have learned) will only ever be comparable to a speck of dust against the universe. <u>You cannot learn how to be non-judgmental, you can only be it.</u> NO

THE COMET

Timeless motion
Drifting into our worldly view.
Interrupting the ever-changing picture.
Demanding attention like the cock in all its' masterful
glory.
It seeks admiration as it travels through it's own ever
changing picture.
Timeless.
Time is contained in a bubble.
It passes.

Message from an Angel

A message from an angel came to me in Jan 2001. It happened like this. My partner and I were driving along a country road in Ireland when three symbols appeared on the side of a mountain. There was a cross, a Star of David (six-pointed star) and a crescent moon in the upright position. We both saw them. I then became aware of a presence, warm and gentle, yet of a very high vibration. I could sense divine energy. The energy struck me as being male. I then became aware that I was being "told" (or having the information impressed onto me), that the presence was my guardian angel whose name is Jason. I stopped in a nearby village where Jason gave me the following message. He asked me to pass this message around the world and to use all modes of communication open to me.

The Message

These symbols are from God (or Source, All-That-Is, Love, Light or whatever name resonates with each individual soul to describe the supreme, eternal power of all existence). The purpose of these symbols is to bring unity to divided minds and to bring peace on Earth and Goodwill (Godwill) to mankind.

These symbols will call forth all the ascended masters Earth has been designated by the combined godheads of *all* religions and belief systems (Jesus, David, Allah, Mohammed, Buddha, Krishna, Zen masters, Sikh masters, Saints, Gurus, etc.). These symbols bring forth (activate) a powerful ray of energy which can be used to open the hearts and minds of humans and to link (ground) the body and soul of each human being with his or her existence on the Earth plane.

The energy or ray to which the symbols are connected is the collective consciousness of the prophets and godheads associated with the symbols (Jesus, David and Allah) and the collective consciousness of all their followers (Christians, Jews and Muslims as well as those of all other belief systems).

To invoke this ray visualise the Cross and say "Jesus, Jesus, Jesus", then visualise the Star of David and say "David, David, David" and visualise the Crescent Moon and say

"Allah, Allah, Allah". * *(Although the prophet was Mohammed, the symbol represents the Sacred Days and is connected to Islam or Allah).*

"JESUS" x 3   "DAVID" x 3   "ALLAH" x 3

Note: If you wish, you could also see a ray of light coming from God, penetrating these symbols, and then carrying them down into the centre of the Earth to be grounded, but this is optional and up to each individual.

The very act of combining these three symbols is an act of unifying the divided mind of humanity and all religious and cultural factions and the divisions that this represents, therefore it is an act of unity. This allows a person to become more themselves; to become as one, united with everybody else, not above or below anybody but equal to all others as human beings – equal as spirits.

If you are limited by your belief system to just one or none of these symbols, they will still work for you if you open yourself to that possibility and allow it to happen. This is not a new faith or belief system or is it ever meant to be in the future. This is about uniting old divisions and healing enmity and separation. Oneness of mind, body and spirit requires no faith or belief – it only requires to be *experienced.*

Outside of the Earth existence these prophets and godheads are united as one. In Truth there are no different "religions" or different "Gods" in the world of spirit. All is one and all is connected to the one source of our existence (and of all existence). There is just one Source – one "Fount of Love" – and we all come from that Source and will inevitably go back to that Source no matter what "religion" or godhead we choose to belong to or follow while on Earth. We will go back to the one true Source because we are all a part of Source and that is where we belong. We will go back despite ourselves and our various deviations into separate pathways (albeit well-intentioned deviations). We will go back to our Source eventually, inevitably, because every atom and particle of everything and everybody/soul issues from, and is intrinsically a part of, Source. There is no separation from the one true Source which is pure Love. This is what is known as "The Oneness" (we are all one). Our purpose in life is to be reunited (re-merged) with our Source. Source/God/Love cannot deny Love to any of its parts for that would be for God to deny God. So our reunion with Source is inevitable no matter how twisted or tortuous or long the journey back.

It is our forefathers and our ancestors who are sending this energy collectively. Those who have gone before us and who left us their legacy of guidelines – each according to their own beliefs while on Earth and within the confines of the rules, rituals and practices of the "Faith" to which they subscribed. They have now reached enlightenment and are the enlightened ones and the masters. They are sending this ray of energy to help us reconcile the differences in our beliefs in God and to give us a tool for healing division and separation and promoting unity and peace, in our hearts and in our world, for our journey back to Source.

When the symbols are used in thought (invoked), word or deed (materialised), they bring the energy ray into action. This ray opens the mind to allow rigid or stuck thought patterns to soften. This allows one to be flexible and eventually open- up to possibilities beyond the limitations, restrictions and divisions handed down from those same forefathers – the restrictions and divisions that we carry today and that we are handing on to our children in our divided communities, countries and world.

In order to rectify our misunderstanding about the one true Source being different godheads and the resulting separation and division this misunderstanding is causing in the world; these same forefathers, now united together as one, are providing humanity at this time with *a simple yet powerful solution* – the unified symbols. It is our misunderstanding about each other as humans rather than our misunderstandings about our godheads that will be rectified.

The three symbols we use each have an equal value or power. It is the way in which we use this power, or the way we value it that empowers the symbol. Words and symbols carry energy. They are like keys to a lock. When words are spoken and symbols drawn or visualised, with intent, in a systematic manner, it produces an effect similar to a combination lock unlocking. As these three symbols are used they will unlock doorways to rooms filled with energy; Love and Light energy which feeds our spirit-self, allowing it to go back to the Light, back to enlightenment.

It cannot hurt anybody if they use these symbols or if the symbols are used by somebody else and sent to them. The three combined symbols can be visualised in the mind and projected on to people, things, places and events with the intention of bringing healing and peace wherever they go. They can be outlined in the air using the hands, a stick of wood, etc., and projected anywhere, to any situation or person. They can be drawn with the fingertips. They can be drawn and painted. They can be used as jewellery, as motifs, etc., – always with the intention of bringing healing and peace wherever and to whomever they go. They can be projected into the television when news of war or fear is being shown. They can be used on the body, in churches, mosques, temples, chapels, and synagogues – anywhere – even on top of mountains. They can be used to heal strife and corruption, violence, disasters, and any event that threatens the balance and/or harmony of individuals, the Earth or humanity. The possibilities are unlimited because *we are all healers.*

Spread the word to the world.

The Power of Symbols

Symbols are very powerful. Their energy can be used as both positive and negative power. However they are used, there will be learning for all that use or follow a symbol. The following is given as an example of the power of the symbol:

The Star of David or the swastika.

The cross has preceded armies against the armies of the Crescent Moon and vice versa.

A plus symbol (+), is interpreted as above or better than a minus.

The white dove has attracted many under its wings of peace.

The pentacle strikes fear in some because of its perceived connection with the "dark forces" *(these words carry negative energy if you allow them to)*.

THE SECOND HAND

Our present becomes past in an instant.
Our future now takes presents' place.
Each moment our moments are changing
And we're changing at the same pace.

CHAPTER EIGHT

Angels

Angels are the only beings that work on all levels of existence or experience in all realities. They take on any form they need to in order for you to feel their unconditional love and beauty. Any form means just that. From the mighty mosquito to the lowly humble beggar in human form. Angels oversee all life. They are of pure love and light. It is through angels that the light comes from Source which is where angels dwell. They carry that love and wisdom, the power and the glory of God, within themselves, giving of themselves unconditionally to all that seek it. Unconditional means just that, without any, (emphasis on "any") conditions whatsoever.

Angels are returning to the Earth in unimaginable numbers or, to put it another way, there is an untapped source of angelic energy waiting to be tapped into by humans. They are patiently and lovingly waiting for you to invite them into your life. Should you do this, you may recognise the energy of an old friend. You are part of that energy weighed down with millennia of matter, the closest to you being your own body or bodies which come together to create the human form. There are bodies you cannot see (this is because you do not look – humanity as a whole has stopped looking). Fear has caused this. Some people *can* see. This number is growing rapidly. You can sense or feel these other bodies through the aura (an energy field within and around all matter). Yes (angels), they do have wings and no, they don't. Any form they need to have, they have-from a grain of salt to a mountain range. From a ball of unseen energy to a beautiful winged being of light. The wings are like an official uniform and are used when needed. Angels can be best likened to the energy of fire.

There are billions of individual fires burning on and in the earth at any one time. Yet all these fires contain the same energy or doing different jobs where needed. In all cases, with all the individual flames, they give out or share energy or power. Humans have tapped into this source of energy on a physical level and can transform it in many ways. Many do not see the spiritual energy within the flame. This energy has carried humanity to new highs and new lows. From the ecstasy of new experiences to the agony of repeating old experiences. The word fire has many connotations or meanings, as has the word angel. If you can open your mind and your thought process to allow for angels to exist, or even the possibility of their existence, you will open a window of opportunity on a soul level. The soul or spirit is contained within the aura, as is the human body. The soul or spirit is made of light – the same energy as angels.

Nothing matters to an angel. That is, nothing that has matter attached to it in anyway, shape or form can have an effect on an angel: they all experience as one. That is, all experiences are shared by all and experienced as one. Their unconditional love means the utmost respect for their own individual free will and that of others, including yours. So be it therefore, you need to ask for their divine intervention, as for angels to intervene without your asking would be a violation of your free will. Angels will work for your highest good and for the highest good of all. That is, what your spirit-self needs, not necessarily what your body or brain (what you think) wants. They will arrange the circumstances for the right conditions at the right time to manifest in order for you to experience what you have chosen to experience in this lifetime (you arranged this before you reincarnated). You do not remember what you have chosen or ordered, but the angels do. They also know that it is the aim of all whom incarnate into the earth experience to achieve total awareness or enlightenment. This is attainable for all that choose it. So be it. It will only happen when you choose it. It will not happen by accident (unless an accident has been chosen). Yes, people choose to have accidents in order to awaken themselves. Ask those who have had a near death experience as they are called. Do they still feel the love now, back in the body, as they did when they were out of the body? Ask about the fear of death or the fear of living, for it is a thin veil that divides these. Their feelings speak their truth. They see the death as a doorway or transition into a new reality.

Just as on earth and in a body, you have free will to experience what you will. In spirit you also have free will to experience what you will in the spirit world. As above, so below. If you will it or believe that angels and loved ones meet you, so be it. If you will it that you enter into a garden or Eden, so be it. If you choose for nothing to happen at the point of death, so be it. Nothing happens. You remain as you are in body, only you will be in spirit. No one will see or hear you except those like-minded spirits (like attracts like), who most likely tell themselves and each other, that they were right. There is no heaven or after-life. This is what they will experience until they choose not to. As the angels work on all levels (dimensions) they will also work with souls who have passed over in whatever way they need to. There is no pain outside the body unless a soul chooses it. A belief in penance, suffering, unworthiness or reparation can cause souls to choose pain.

Angels create the circumstances for our birth and our death. They are over-seeing an unseen workforce of spirit beings of all shapes, colours and sizes and building the collective reality as humans will it. The greatest good of all is their mission. So, if a spirit who has chosen to incarnate as part of a bigger group in order to gain an experience that will create change for the greater good, then wills to alter that experience, his angel will create the circumstances that keeps him tied or bonded with his mission. If through spiritual healing, these ties or bonds are cut and the person is unaware of his mission or chosen experience in life, he will find himself attaching to another group with the same purpose. This may be interpreted as not being able to escape from ones destiny, fate or karma (which is spiritual awareness, enlightenment or oneness) e.g. if it is more beneficial for a spirit to live a life of poverty within a larger group, and experience starvation in order to leave the body or die, as it is called. Since this is your chosen path, you will never get a break or chance to improve your situation until the above scenario plays itself out. This is the reality for countless millions of spirits over countless lifetimes or incarnations, all lovingly and unconditionally manifested by angels. The same can be said for the experience of a life of material wealth and so-called luxury. This is also the reality for countless millions of spirits over countless lifetimes or incarnations. Each lifetime embodies an aspect of the same spirit (soul part) coming and going from one experience to another, time and time again. Each lifetime is an opportunity for spiritual growth towards awareness regardless of the duration. Angels will do all in their power to help a soul achieve this through their limitations of the physical, emotional and mental states. They can only do for us, what we will them to do, no more or no less.

The earth is a point of interaction where beings of higher and lower vibrations can mix freely. Those of higher vibrations are spirits who have evolved or enlightened more (the rate of purity at which energy is flowing) and those of lower vibration are others who may have had as many experiences yet may not have found as much enlightenment or awareness. The point of awareness or enlightenment reached on earth in a lifetime determines the level you will exist on outside of that lifetime. The natural order of this universe and its' law of "like to like", means that, beings of like- mindedness or vibration come together in a seemingly layered or hierarchical order: the heaviest or enlightened at the bottom and the lightest or most enlightened at the top, with various levels in-between. In truth there is no separation, The only difference that exists in the spirit world is in levels of awareness of love. All are contained within the oneness (love) from the so-called archangels to the mischievous earth-bound, stubborn old ghost. The angels, with unconditional love, try to help us to create our own reality no matter what that may be whatever our level of existence.

The hierarchical structure within the realms of angels exists so as to avoid chaos. All are equal, pure love is just that. Angels have different roles or functions. Archangels and others with titles are like overseers or managers. They direct the angels to whoever or wherever they are needed, for the highest good of all. Similar to the elements of earth having their own specific purpose (to inter act and react within the confines of the atmosphere that has been created), there are natural laws or spiritual or universal laws that these elements adhere to. Fire and water, air and earth, above and below, function independently only within the perfect circumstances. Outside of that you would have chaos. Under the watchful eyes of the angels and through the angels to the spirits of the elements (or elementals), the natural order is created. If the spirit of the air merges into fire, water or earth, it ceases to be air and becomes what it has merged with. Or fire, when merged with water, ceases to be fire. The spirit of the fire passes over into the spirit world of water and into another experience in its' continual existence.

All angels are aware that they are of the highest and purest expression of unconditional love, they have no sense of having to achieve a level of perfection. They *are* that level of perfection and therefore can work within realms of vibration (the rate at which divine energy is flowing) lower and denser than themselves, without these vibrations affecting them. In fact they raise the vibration of all that their energy touches.

For angels to work with humans they need to be *asked* (ask and thou shall receive). They will allow you (if you will allow them) to feel their energy, unconditional love and peace through meditation and awareness of their presence.

INNER-VOICE

We are all fallen angels,
On a journey back to light.
Caught up in earthly cycles,
As we try to get it right.

There is no end to chances earned,
With each successive life.
Become aware of who you are,
A beautiful being of light.

Change your personal agenda,
And you can have the might,
Of the universe behind you.
We're waiting here to guide you.

The answers lie inside - you.
Have to quiet your mind,
To listen to a voice, who
Is already a part of - you.
Must balance what you listen to,
Your ego or to me.

EXERCISE TO MEET YOUR ANGEL

Use incense, candles and soft music. Create a pleasant atmosphere.

Sit in a comfortable position, feet touching the floor.

Clear your energy field with white light breathing.

Mentally ask your guides to help you connect with your angel.

Relax in this energy for a few minutes.

Visualise a silver cord or beam of light coming out from the back of your head at the base of your skull.

Imagine the cord passing through the ceiling.

Follow this out into the sky, up through the clouds into the higher atmosphere, out into space.

Now see a star in the distance.

Move toward the star.

See the silvery white light getting brighter and brighter as you approach.
Look beyond the star.

See the sun in the distance.

See a ray of golden white light coming from the sun towards you.

Let it touch you.

Move back toward the star bringing the golden ray with you, in you, back into the silvery white light of the star.

Let it touch you.

Move back down the silvery cord bringing both rays, silver and gold, with you, in you.

Back through the higher atmosphere, down through the sky, the clouds, into the room.

Feel the surge of energy as the light enters through the base of your skull.

Allow it to flow through you, out of you, through your aura.

Sit here in this energy of love, allow what will happen to happen.

Do not pre-empt or expect. Take a back seat.
Allow it to unfold in whatever way it will.
Stay here for as long as you wish to.

You will feel a sense of power and peace.

Some people sense a feeling of being ten feet tall and an exhilaration that words are inadequate to describe. Some see, some hear, some sense the angels. Some just know. When you are ready, thank your angel and guides. See the silver and gold rays disconnecting from you. Visualise or imagine your aura closing in around you like a protective bubble or shell. Reinforce your connection with the earth by pushing down on your feet, physically and mentally.

SPIRIT GUIDES

Spirit guides are like parents. We all have them. They exist whether or not we know them, communicate with them, whether we can see them, be with them or whether or not we love or believe in them. They exist.

The very presence of those who have passed before us proves that life continues after death (though proof is not needed). They are guides to our spirit - self, not just guides who happen to be in spirit form and so we must open our mind and heart to our own spirit self to communicate with and access this guidance (spirit-to-spirit). Like with our parents, we choose (where choice is available) whether or not we listen to them or take their guidance, help, opinions or any lessons they may have taught or have to teach us. The same is true of your spirit guides, except here choice is always available.

Like most parents, they protect and guide us through some of our life experiences, except the spirit guide knows our life experience goes beyond this present existence. This is what their guidance is based on, the continuation of life. This is to what and where they are guiding us as guides.

Guides are spirits who have been here, done that, got the t-shirt. They have lived on earth in a body, as you are doing now. They choose to return a part of themselves to help others to help themselves. They see a bigger picture so to speak. They know what you, your spirit-self or soul-self came here to experience. They work and live outside of time and avail of every opportunity to impress on you what you need to know or experience in order for you to choose what you need to know or experience. They are beings of light as you and I are. As you let their light guide yourself, you too shine your light unto others, teaching by example.

ONE AT A TIME

One at a time,
we stand in line.
One at a time,
we are born.
One at a time,
we learn, we grow.
One at a time,
we are enlightened, we know.
One at a time,
we are destined to go.
One at a time,
our heart beats, our breaths inhaled,
our eyes meet, we grieve, we feel pain.
One at a time, we heal
or we do it all over again.

CHAPTER NINE

ARCHANGEL MICHAEL

There has been much talk of massive changes to the atmospheres of the planet earth with dire predictions being forecast, creating fear. Because people do not see a threat to their own existence in the immediate future, this fear is being projected into the distant future, into the void. It is being added to and is beginning to take form. This is the view from above (the higher dimensions), from a point where all possibilities can be seen and to which possibilities, thought-forms both positive and negative, are attaching themselves and are being made manifest. Because you are co-creators with the source of all and you use your thoughts to create. Fearful thoughts bring fearful experiences, loving thoughts bring loving experiences, individually and collectively. This is "thy will be done on earth". If you respond with fear to these predictions you will energise them into reality. If you respond with love (send light to them) you will transmute or change them. Humanity as a whole has the power through free will and choice to create your future as it will enfold.

The earth, as a spiritual being containing energies and light forms beyond mere human comprehension or existence, is itself working at an ever changing level of vibration, adjusting accordingly to the highest good of all (not just humans). Earth has raised its' vibrations. Many who have incarnated as light workers have been raising their vibrations in order for more beings of higher vibration to connect to the earth. This has been achieved.

What has been talked about as the "eighth ray", has been anchored and grounded into reality. There is now in place around the earth, a ball of pure love, which can be accessed by all. It is part of the divine plan and has always been available. In your past, few accessed this. Now in your present, many are spiritually aware. It is this awareness that has drawn this energy of pure love closer to earth.

The eighth ray is centred deep inside the earth and vibrating outward releasing long-time, stuck energy blocks to the surface where they will have to be faced and addressed. The beginnings of a new world-order are already starting to form. Old extremist belief systems are dissolving. Single or closed-minded, old world-order, institutions, religions, even countries and borders are coming to a close. They have served their purpose. The collective consciousness or mindset of those connected with these institutions, government's etc., has changed, allowing for new experiences to enter into their reality. This, which was once only a possibility, has taken form and is now a reality. It was foreseen and predicted. It has been called the Christ consciousness. This expression narrows its' importance. The Christ consciousness has merged with the body or energy mass of the creator and re-emerged as one aspect of a collective consciousness or energy numbering billions of beings of light. These are known as the masters, the ascended masters or enlightened ones. This level of existence is to where all of our souls will eventually return. It is where over-souls exist. It is not limited to human or earth experience. It is from this consciousness/level of existence that the eighth ray is coming. This is in accordance with the divine plan: "Thy will be done on earth". This is where those who are deemed as saints or prophets exist as one (in one-ness). From Mother Mary to Krishna, from Mohammed to Buddha and from Jesus to Moses. These are the names for one earth existence only of individual soul aspects that are now returned with their over-soul. They have ascended to merge with all souls who have reached full awareness – "like to like".

As earth' vibrations were raising, earth was also healing and growing. The earth, like humans, has energy points like chakras. As with humans, these energy points can get clogged or broken through negative energy, activities or thought forms. This results in dis-ease or disharmony and illness. People are being used as energy points all around the world. Healers and spiritualists are radiating energy keeping the balances balanced. People who come into contact with these light workers will themselves radiate energy thereby becoming part of the balance.

"Perfectly balanced" in the spirit-sense or spirit world is not as on earth. This is not open to debate, interpretation or personal or collective agenda. "Balance" in the spirit sense is a continuing experience with no gaps, vacuums or voids. You are aware of the energy flowing in and around you and you are aware of yourself consciously adding to that energy. This is balance and it can be love or fear as chosen e.g. there are vast numbers of discarnate spirits dwelling or existing or experiencing a place they commonly call hell or the underworld. For whatever reasons (and each spirit has its own reason) their sense of unworthiness, guilt or fear results from unaware thought processes or actions while on earth. When reviewed after the leaving of the body, their core belief systems believe they should be punished. They believe this is how it should be or will be. So be it. This is not negative, bad or wrong. It is not evil. It is simply a state of be-ing resulting from a state of mind, a new experience and perfectly balanced. As are all realms of existence (which number many) between heaven (total awareness, oneness) and hell, unawareness and separation. The same state of being can be achieved in a lifetime on earth. It can be heaven or it can be hell. As above, so below.

The process of developing a thought into matter or an idea into reality takes time here on earth. This is the only place that the concept of time exists. Outside of the body in spirit or in the spirit world, there is no time and so, no time for a developing process. Thoughts and ideas are experienced instantaneously. You think it, you feel it, see it, taste it, hear it, smell it, whatever the "it", you experience it with all your being. It is as real as it appears or manifests, to those who experience it, as the earth is to those with a body or within the confines of time.

Wise spirits or those aware that thoughts manifest, choose their thoughts carefully. Just as a person on earth encounters boundaries built by belief systems of the collective (group energy), so it is in spirit. Collective boundaries can exist and seem real to those who choose to experience them. "Like attracts like". Vast numbers of soul parts exist in separate heavens (Catholic, Jewish and Muslim etc.), content to be receiving their perceived, "just" rewards. These experiences of different heavens are created by boundaries that keep them apart, so the illusion of separation is experienced both on earth and in the spirit world. A spirit or soul part can leave any level of experience in an instant if it wills it from the centre of its being. Which involves thinking beyond the boundaries. The level of existence or experience to which it evolves is open ended within the natural law of "like to like". However, it cannot exist in full awareness or oneness until it becomes fully aware.

Levels of awareness or light levels in the being, be it with or without a physical body, manifest as vibrations. These range from dense or dull and slow moving through to light and rapidly moving. This creates stratas or different levels of light and like layers of sand, stones, pebbles and rocks, each strata will find its' own level, the lightest at the top and heaviest at the bottom. The heavy rock cannot rise to the top until it has changed into sand. "Like to like" or gravity as it is called. Each stratum gravitates towards itself. All are part of the same substance; sand and rock etc., being earth, yet they exist at different levels.

The spirit world viewed in this way reflects a perception of a hierarchical structure or ladder. It is not. It is this way in order for the reality of the earth experience to exist.

THE EARTH EXPERIENCE

Angels are beings of light or balls of pure, unconditional love that evolved out of love itself. This, the source of love from which they evolved, has been called God or Source. The angels, like the source or being they evolved from, are eternal with no beginning or end. This is not an easy concept for the limited human brain but it can be comprehended by an open mind. Angels are comprised of love energy, which is God. This love energy is forever recharging itself with its' own energy and growing in awareness of itself and forever creating new experiences by the power of thought.

The first angels were created by Source (God) in order that Source (God) could have the experience of sharing. Source (God or light) expanded itself into billions upon billions of angels, thereby sharing billions upon billions of experiences simultaneously. So it was, is now and ever shall be. These others in turn, created others, each with the same ability as Source, each a mirror image of itself, each with its' own free will. This free will is sacrosanct. It cannot deny itself its' own free will and love, which is unconditional love. And so the angels also recreated themselves. They were one with God since all were comprised of the same God essence. What one experienced they all experienced simultaneously, yet at the same time each individual angel (or aspect of God) has the free will to experience what it wills. Which simply means, the answer to any request i.e. thought or idea from an angel or any soul, can never be no as all will is from Source or God's will, freely and unconditionally given to itself. All life forms stem from a single cell which divides and sub-divides over and over during the course of it's life cycle. The single cell is God.

One angel thought of separation as a new experience. This was a part of God, a part of oneness, choosing to experience what it is like not to be a part of God or oneness. And so it was. A new order had to be created to experience this separation. Each angel agreed to this, as not to agree would have been to deny its' own free will. So by the power of thought they created the universe and planet earth, with their very being, their light bodies or individual minds. The angels merged together in order to form a universe that would sustain the earth. They had to lower their vibration or light level in order to achieve a denser form/energy that would allow the formation of this new universe and of planet earth. To experience the separation, they had to be different, in order to be different they would have to create an illusion. For no thing, including God can be a different thing than itself. And so an illusion was created.

You, the universe, planet earth and the separation from God are all illusions. The way out of the illusion was and is the same as the way it was created – by the power of thought. The loving thought of oneness is all that was and is required to end the illusion and be reunited with Source. The illusion is but a thought of an angel, an angel daydreaming, the same as you dream and experience your dream as reality and those you encounter in your dream seem real to you yet you do not remember most of it when you (seem to) wake up. This world called earth is but a dream within a dream. You are more than just a body on a planet floating in space. You are an aspect of Source/God having a dream, a spiritual being using this world and body to awaken yourself to that fact.

The first angels merged together and became the earth itself with all of its' elements. They separated themselves into the elemental spirits. Others created their own different life forms. Still others came to live as residents of this atmosphere that was creating itself. The first residents came as beings of light without a body and existed on this plane for what is now called millions of years, in that state of being. All had a deep sense of knowing that it really was and is an illusion. They knew who and what they really were.

Over vast periods of time and evolution, other thoughts and more separation created the human form. This form had to be born into the illusion with no recollection of ever having been an angel. In this way the illusion was and is, lived as reality to this day. The angels withdrew out of sight leaving the human aspect seemingly alone or separate, with no memory on the physical level of its' overall experience or of its' over-soul or soul-self (also called higher self).

The first humans used all their senses for survival. They could see auras and elemental spirits. They lived in harmony with nature and could feel and sense disharmony and heal it in the earth and each other. They lived in communities of extended families where all were equal.

Knowledge was shared and free will was respected. The concept of imposing ones will onto another had not been thought of.

The angels did not desert the earth or truly separate from their physical aspect. They merely withdrew from sight within the illusion of separation. So humans, though unaware, had and still have the ability to bring their thoughts into creation and into reality just like angels and God. The thoughts themselves take shape without human interference. Humans are a conduit for the thoughts. Thoughts only have to pass through the mind for this is where thoughts derive power. The longer a thought is held in the mind, the more powerful it becomes. This is what turns possibilities into reality. The more minds that hold the same thought, the stronger the possibility gets. It then becomes a probability and eventually evolves into a reality. The place or level where thoughts and possibilities exist is called the void or space. Thoughts/ solutions/ ideas, seem to come from nowhere. The void or space is universal energy.

This is energy that does not control how or what it is used for. It is detached from what it creates with its' own energy. This energy can be likened to a huge storehouse or warehouse of components. Thoughts connected to emotions is how we order from this storehouse. Our guardian angel can be likened to the warehouse/ storehouse assistant who delivers your order, be it in spare parts or separate components for building over time, or they can deliver the complete order at once, whichever is for the highest good of all.

The first humans lived very long life times not knowing fear or guilt. Their connections to the elemental spirits led them to ask questions which came as thought-forms in their minds (a puzzling event for early humans, who were acting on instinct without question). Birth, life and death (rebirth) were as acceptable as the will to survive. Like day and night, it just was. There was no spoken language. They used all their senses including the ability to read each other's auras, to detect moods and feelings. There was no shame and nothing was hidden. Sounds were limited to warnings or to seek others attention. Also when pleasure and pain were experienced, some, through their contact with the elementals, experienced (through meditation or stillness) the ability to leave the body and enter the world of the elementals. Here they learned about organisation, as these spirits are highly evolved beings. They also learned about planting, growing and harvesting of food and were told or shown what was good to eat or what was poisonous. This information was shared and passed from one generation to another. This was happening simultaneously in seven different locations on earth. The first humans were the original tribes of humanity placed on earth as part of the divine plan. Two in the Americas, one in Europe, one in Asia, one in Australia and two in Africa. These original seven primitive tribes expanded in numbers and locations as their knowing grew and as their ability to process thoughts in the mind developed or evolved. From the elementals they learned about fire, cooking, fishing and hunting. It was in these realms or state of being that early humans saw angels. It was also on these journeys that fear was encountered, experienced and shared. They were expanding their experiences/ awareness beyond anything and everything already known. Some early humans had the ability to travel or journey out of their bodies into the spirit world. As they travelled in spirit they met others, similar yet different to themselves, who were also resident on planet earth but were also journeying into the spirit world. These new beings had different eyes, hair, skin colour, facial features and strange environments. On returning to their tribes after their spirit journeys, these first humans acted out their experiences or described them through dance and drama. Each observer and participant interpreting the experience in their own limited way. This led to the first experiences of fear, which gathered as a mass of negative energy (fearful thought forms). This mass of negative energy went into the void. All thought forms positive and negative automatically entered the void.

Through these encounters in spirit, the seven tribes feared each other long before they had physically seen each other. With fear, over time, came the concept of greed and other never before thought of experiences. In turn, these led to thoughts of possessiveness, guilt, anger, shame and the concept of imposing ones will over another. These thoughts were energised or fed by the fear within the void and evolved into human reality. The rest is humanities history: a history of conflict and greed. This is existence on the physical level.

As the original first humans of the seven tribes passed back into spirit form e.g. those who had succeeded in living in harmony with their surroundings and other human beings, re emerged with their higher - self (the angel from which they had first emerged) the earth experience was complete. Humanity is the continuation of the illusion of separation. All became as one again and in so doing, their individual experiences also became as one with all and they became aware of the experiences of all others. All were in agreement that the earth experience had brought to the collective as a whole, oneness/ God. A sense of rejoicing: of joy repeating itself. This was a new experience for it was love reunited with itself and feeling it billions upon billions of times simultaneously. An overwhelming, ecstatic and empowering state of being. These mere descriptive words cannot even begin to define it. It is the ultimate of spiritual experiences to which all souls will eventually be reunited. This is awareness – "oneness" at a higher level. It is beyond the level of possibilities open to the human experience. It cannot be experienced fully while a spirit is in a human body. Although glimpses or tastes can be experienced by humans.

As the following generations of the tribes (who had been born of man and woman) passed into spirit, their disincarnate spirit moved towards the angels who greeted them. They became aware of the true nature of their being and their connection and inter-connection with all others – a process known as the life review – not just the human or physical life, but also the spiritual life.

With awareness came the knowing that angels are pure love and, as like attracts like, only some of those who had been born passed into the realms of angels. The universal law of return (what you give, so shall you receive) is exact. All thoughts or actions born of fear or negative energy that had not been resolved on earth were now presented to the now aware, returned spirit (or aspect of an angel), as were all thoughts and actions of love. All experiences are held in the memory. The spirit is now in a state of self-assessment. Here you ask yourself if you are of the purity of love (like to like) to merge with all, or if your purity has been tainted with that which is not love or fear. No one stands in judgement. Love cannot deny itself. Each spirit measures or weighs its own levels of love and fear. One act of love can out-weigh many acts or experiences of fear, as can one act or experience of fear can out-weigh many of love.

This level of existence is also a new experience as you become aware of your light level or how much love or awareness of love you still are. You exist on that level with others of like-mindedness or light level. Friendships and bonds are formed here. Soul mates and soul-groups also form. As free will is eternal, a spirit or group of spirits make their own choices about how they will proceed. Angels who work to assist us at all levels, are available for help and advice. It is also the level where reincarnation is available. A soul can choose to come to earth-life again, to try the experience again and face any fears or negative thought forms that remained from the last or previous incarnations (this is know as Karma). The spirit does not return itself, but sends an aspect of itself, just as the angels did. The new aspect (or person) simply emerges from the soul as a being of light (thereby forming a soul family or over-soul) complete with all the awareness or knowing of itself. Together, they (the different soul aspects, angels and guides if chosen) plan a new lifetime, from the physical shape right through to how it will re-emerge (or die) from the experience.

REINCARNATION

At birth, the first breath, the being of light merges with the physical, mental and emotional bodies. All previous memories are blocked or forgotten. This is a continuing cycle until one of these aspects becomes aware of who and what they are while incarnated in a body. This will enable the entire soul family (which can number few or many aspects of the one soul) to merge with the aspect incarnated on earth. This process involves the human aspect facing the fears that other aspects of their over-soul or higher self did not overcome and then facing them and overcoming them with love. This only happens when you are ready for it. These are seen as challenges, tests, missions or karma. The way in which a person acts, feels and reacts to the trials and tribulations of a lifetime determine the outcome. What of the souls or their aspects who do not reach awareness while on earth? The cycle continues with over-souls and soul groups working together in the spirit world (or "heaven" as it is sometimes called). They send aspects to earth or incarnate in groups working on the fear and experiencing it so that an aspect or aspects of the same soul group can experience the circumstances that produced the fear and overcome it with love. In simple terms, everything happens for a reason. There are no coincidences. All that happens is meant to happen and the reason is simply to find love for yourself and your brother, sister or fellow human beings. Souls agree to help each other to do this in ones, twos, family groups, communities, so-called ethnic groups and nationalities. They do this with the full awareness that the physical body is only a vehicle or tool to an end and will be discarded in the process of spiritual growth. This is achieved by means of reflection. That is, when a person, family group, community etc. is affected in a negative way i.e. fear, hate, judgement, seeking to control or revenge, by another person, family or community etc., it is a reflection of the same issues within that person, group, community etc., that needs to be focused on and healed. The divine plan is that all will find love and all will merge as one again. There will be an aspect of all seeking full awareness until it is reached for all. Where and how each aspect seeks it is open to free will, whether in a body or not. There is no time limit. We have eternity.

Eureka! You have reached ascension, nirvana, heaven and paradise. But what next for the soul? For this is not where a merger with all oneness occurs, even though the sense of rejoicing and love are immense and shared by all at this level (like to like). Here, while still an individual soul, you are connected to collective consciousness. This collective consciousness is fully aware. This means all that exist at this level know what is being written here. What this collective wants is to help others to achieve this level for we are all one and we gladly and lovingly wait and send assistance in every imaginable way to those other souls who are following behind us. For to progress further into the light would be an unaware action or an unaware thought, the thought of separation. Between the levels of full awareness and certainty, there are many levels of unawareness and uncertainty. The first or lowest of these levels is that of fear. The levels have been called astral planes, dimensions and levels of existence and are known as "bardos" in Buddhism. There is no set number of levels as each individual spirit has the ability to create its' very own level. Because of the order of things within the universal laws, these levels have been contained within the structure of seven over-all levels. The eighth ray has expanded this to eight levels. Beyond the eighth ray lie the realms of the angels, oneness and source, which are also structured at varying levels. Those on the eighth level are free to enter the upper levels. These levels are beyond human comprehension and will cause fear in those who insist on entering them or accessing information from them, for they will pass into the Great Void. This is a place where all the possibilities for the rest of "what is" exist. The human experience is just one of an infinite number of experiences of "what is". By entering the great void a person can become attached to possibilities which are not for the human experience

The earth or human experience has its own void where all possibilities exist that relates to humanity or earth. This is not the great void.

It is not advisable for humans to enter the great void on the higher levels just as it would not be advisable to allow a child to play with petrol and matches, yet at a later stage of development it may be quite safe. This is not a boundary or rule. Humans have been travelling into this great void ever since they connected with the elementals. But they travelled in the company of angels and of the masters. They went as observers or guests, for many have been taken to these places either while sleeping or in meditation. This is a spontaneous occurrence and not as a result of intention. The masters and the angels in conjunction with your higher self choose who and when. Nothing that exists in the great void can ever happen on earth. Those who seek to enter without an invitation may enter at will and return with impossible dreams and/or fear of impossibilities (all things are possible between heaven and earth). The great void is beyond heaven. There is no way a spirit or person in meditation or sleep-state can accidentally enter the great void. Clear intentions, determination and desire are needed. A desire for knowledge (a need to understand within the limitations of the logical brain) which is distinct from knowing. Knowing needs no understanding as knowing is awareness and a spiritual quality. All of "what is", simply is, with or without human understanding of the complexities of the process. For that which gives life (the power supply, the source of all-that-is), cannot be understood, only experienced.

Spirit time is non existent. It is difficult for humans to comprehend existence in other worlds or levels outside of earth time. Even within their own world, most humans don't see the spiritual aspect of everything – the spiritual aspect of life itself and all the life that is around them, every word spoken, every thought formed and every action taken.

Even when humans experience travelling to other places while in an altered or dream state, where sometimes they see loved ones who have crossed over into spirit, where long distances are covered in seconds, where they can sense and experience joy and fear, where they seem to be immortal, even waking up just before the point of death, most humans don't see the spiritual aspect.

All humans dream, all spirit and soul aspects can travel out of the body and do so at every opportunity.

This book offers you the tools to do this in a conscious state. It is an answer to the silent cry, the cry from the spirit within for guidance. To those who seek miracles or proof, the proof is in the miracle of each and every moment. Life is the miracle – all life (not just human life), down to the tiniest particle your science can measure. Even the substance called air that you breathe, is a life form. Life is not a gift to humans to enjoy or destroy. Humans are part of life – all life.

MIND CONTROL

We catch a thought and mould it in our mind,
to suit our own perspective.
Examine and you'll find
a whole array of possibilities,
struggling to find, an attachment to the thought.
To be the one that's right for now,
to fertilise and show you how,
to bring it to fruition.
Like a moment of conception,
pre-conceived suggestions.
Turn this thought into a question.
Why, what, where, when?
If's and but's.
What then has the thought become?
A worry, stress or fear?
If it has, just let it go and it will disappear.
Or will it stay?
Thoughts have just the power we give them.
When we catch them they take hold
and they grow as we feed to them.
They do exactly as they're told.
Turn happy, sad, good or bad.
They are in your mind, who's in control.
Thoughts are linked into our feelings.
They are the start of every dream.
They are the substance of real nightmares.

They are the seed to everything.
If you think you can't, you won't.
If you cannot think then you don't.
Then your feelings will adjust like a chemical reaction.
They change because they must.
The feeling of fear can be numbing,
caught naked in the cold and the dark.
You summoned it there by thinking afraid,
a natural protection to keep us alert.
And you can send it back by thinking, relax.
Adjust your own feelings,
select what you think.
Between the thought and the feeling,
you are the link.

CHAPTER TEN

ARCHANGEL GABRIEL ON DEATH

When you die, that is, when you leave the body and return to spirit, you cannot bring the body with you. What you are is what you bring with you. What are you? Who you are at present will fade with time, but what you are abides – is eternal. So, what are you? This is what you are not – you are not your body. You are not any image of how you see yourself. You are not your brain. You are not any idea of who you think you are or of how much knowledge you have acquired. You are not your family and any sense of belonging to a structured, safe framework is not you. You are not what you do, where you live, how much money you make, spend, save or give away. You are not what you look like or how you behave or speak. In fact you are nothing of which forms your reality in this material world (what you can see, smell or touch). None of the things that are part of your present surroundings or circumstances are taken with you.

What you are and take with you, is your response. How you respond to these outer surroundings and your feelings and the emotions that trigger off your feelings. You will find that your feelings and emotions are yours. They are you. They don't belong to anyone else or to any thing outside of you.

Justice and judgement belong to you. You will judge yourself. There is no avenging angel. There is no retribution going to be exacted from you by any other force. The first realisation or revelation you will experience is that life continues. You will discover that you are not dead but very much alive. You will then realise the second revelation – that you are an individual with free will (even if you pass over to spirit as part of a group i.e. plane crash, war, earth quake, flood etc.). No one or no thing will force you into any actions or decisions or tell you where to go or what to do.

You will become aware of the light. A vortex or doorway of light (also known as "the tunnel") will be available to you. If you choose to enter the light, this will take you out of the earth experience. The choice is up to you. You make the choice of whether or not you enter the light. Choosing not to enter the light will not bring life back to the body you occupied. You will remain earth-bound as a spirit until you choose to enter the light. Since there is no time in the spirit world you will have no sense of time, you will soon realise that you do not have to eat or drink in order to live. You will also realise that you still have feelings but that you are no more than your feelings. There is no substance to your being except feelings. While you remain earth bound you will retain your thought process. You will realise that the entire material world that your body occupied was and is an illusion. You will find that you are able to pass through matter i.e. walls and doors etc. If you think of somebody or some place, you will be there instantly for you are only your thoughts or feelings. You will only experience what your mind (dictated to by its thought process), allows you to. You may limit yourself to what and where you think you belong and to what you think belongs to you; a family, a house or land, a car or job. In fact, you may live just as you did when you had a body. No one will hear or see you except other earth bound spirits (if your mind allows it) and some psychics, most of whom will have little to do with you except to offer you the choice to enter the light. Some people may sense you as an uncomfortable energy or presence and most may choose not to occupy the same space as you. You are in a state of disbelief. You do not believe or accept that you have passed over into spirit or died. Millions remain earthbound. Those who had no interest in their spiritual nature while in a body will not suddenly become interested in it when they pass over or leave the body. If you have no time for your spiritual nature (who and what you really are) while your body and mind exist in the earth experience, you most certainly do not have "time" after your body ceases to exist. Once you become spirit again, the concept of time is no longer part of your reality. Even if you do choose to remain earth bound, seconds, minutes, hours, days, weeks, months, years, decades and even centuries will mean nothing to you. You will remain in the same state of ignorance to your true nature as you were in the moment you passed over. There is not a force or power that can change your mind or would be even remotely interested in attempting to change your mind.

Change must be a free-will choice made from within. You will still have your guides and guardian angels to help and assist you, but if you are oblivious to them while you "lived" in your body, you will remain oblivious to them after you pass over, until you consciously seek or ask their help. As above, so below (it is the same for every spirit, with or without the body). So here in this state you will remain until you choose to decide to move towards the light.

The light or "the tunnel" remains as a very vivid memory to the earth bound spirit and will keep on presenting itself to your mind. Guides will repeatedly show their light and love by appearing to you. Also, you can be helped to move towards the light if another aspect of your soul becomes aware or enlightened while in a body as this releases all passed lives from whatever state, level or bardo they exist in and on. It is fear that prompts or stops a spirit from entering the light. An example of this would be an over-soul that has sent many aspects of itself to incarnate on earth over many lifetimes and on different pathways i.e. nationality, religion, sexuality, war, peace etc. Yet none of these aspects found or experienced unconditional love for itself and all others and so these aspects are scattered within the different realms of existence in the spirit world i.e. Hindu heaven, hell because of guilt, Catholic heaven, earth bound through fear and stubbornness etc. The over-soul then decides to send two aspects as brothers within a family. The over-soul meets with the over-soul of the parents and the life paths of the children are planned. Included in this plan is a car accident in which one of the brothers is killed or returns to spirit form and his passing over has such an effect on the other brother that it changes his life and sets him onto a spiritual path. If this aspect or brother goes on to find unconditional love on this path (even if it is only for a moment) and is aware of it, the instant he becomes aware of this, all the other aspects automatically leave the realm of existence they are experiencing or stuck on and return to the over-soul. This is not a violation of free will as it is what the over-soul wants and is for the greater good of all.

All who live on earth are representing all those who have gone before them. All have the knowing of enlightenment within. All have the choice of how and where to spend their time.

FEAR

The fear can manifest in many ways and be disguised as anger, bitterness, possessiveness, guilt, vengeance, pride turned to stubbornness, self-righteousness, blame, victimisation, powerlessness and loneliness. The list is ongoing with new words being invented to cover or mask that which cannot be covered or masked. Those who experience fear (it is manifested as any or the entire previous list) know at the core of themselves that they are fearful. They can feel it, see it, sense it and taste it. They can touch it as it touches them. This fear is an energy that they project to others from behind the mask. People or spirits that are fearful within them will be fearful of another or others who are fearful within them. They will be attracted towards themselves (like to like). This occurs in order for them to see the fear – their own fear reflected back from the significant other or others.

All is well, for through the darkness of fear, the light of love can be seen. All of the above is part of the earth experience. Which ultimately is for spirit to find love for itself – unconditional love that has no boundaries, so, love for itself without boundaries means unconditional love for all that seems outside of itself. This ultimately means love for itself is love for all that is not itself.

The ultimate fear faced within the illusion of the earth experience is that of death. This manifests itself as fear of the death of your family or partner, friends, community, religion, culture, country, race, civilisation, yourself and all that you see as attachments. These are what you are tied or bonded to. The boundaries you build around yourselves; the boundaries that ensure conflict will continue (like to like) within the family, with your partner or so-called friends. Boundaries that keep communities, religions, so-called races, cultures, countries and civilisations apart. More than apart, against one another, as enemies.

Fear is your greatest enemy and your greatest enemies or enemy brings you your greatest victory-love. Love your enemy and you will find love for yourself. Justice and judgement are yours, only for you, not others. This is free will. Your earth experience is yours. You, not others, are totally responsible for how you choose to experience it with your free will. You make your choices each moment. This is the most valuable opportunity open to you to find love. Each and every moment of every millisecond, hour or day, you have free will to choose, change and to choose love. It can overcome your fear. It will overwhelm your perceived enemy-fear. Your own fear. "Do unto others, as you would have others do unto you". The law of return is exact. What you give, so shall you receive. Every moment is an opportunity for spiritual growth.

When moments stop, when you pass over back to spirit and you enter into the light, you will feel peaceful and light (that is, without weight). Any physical pain will be gone and you will feel loved (any preconceived expectations will be experienced). Guides will greet those without expectations. Most spirits are unprepared for their passing into spirit and so most pass in a state of shock or confusion or in a dazed state if drugs were involved. The spirit body or etheric body will be whole and in working order (no matter in what state the physical). Each will be taken to a place of beauty and serenity of their own design. The guides know what an individual requires. Here you will dwell until you adjust to your new state of being.

Realisations and revelations come instantly. This is your inner knowing revealing itself and you realise who and what you really are. When you have adjusted, family or loved ones will visit you (if you have not expected this). If you had, they will already be with you. Any ties or bonds and any worries about unfinished business that you still have with the earth will be presented to your mind. Again the realisation will be instant. These ties and bonds, people, things or issues, are no longer part of you or who you are. You are now in a state of acceptance and you release all remaining energy belonging to your earth existence, for you will know the truth. You cannot take it with you because none of these people, things or issues are actually part of you and in your new state of acceptance, that's ok. You are at ease and as the earth energy leaves, it is replaced with love. This is not new energy coming in. It is simply your true nature emerging and you become aware again of who and what you are.

You will experience this, not simply know it as in knowledge. You will feel it and sense it. You will be it. The "it" is love and you will love it. All who enter into the light will experience love without exception and the light will be offered to all that are born into the earth experience without exception. As above, so below. You will be aware of what it is to be fully aware.

You will also be aware of the life review, the law of return. You will see, meet and know your guides because your energy is now love, unconditional love of self and all others who are also love. You have no sense of self-preservation. Your guides take you to meet your guardian angel and other highly evolved beings of light (these have evolved or enlightened through purification beyond the need for the etheric body). These are sometimes called the Lords of Karma. These are not here to judge you. Again, justice and judgement are yours and here is where you become fully aware of that. This is your life review. In the loving presence of the divine energy of these beings and angels, you will be aware of every thought that you clung to and how you felt, every word spoken and how you felt, every action taken and how you felt. You will see all others as spirits, the same as you. You will feel as they did, for you will be aware of oneness. You enter into the realm of the lords of karma as a fully aware being. You merge with your over-soul. All your experiences are held within your over-soul, including the ones being reviewed. It is how you lived the earth experience that determines your level of awareness. If and when you leave the lords of karma, you will exist with others at your level of awareness. "Thy will be done on earth as it is in heaven". As "thy will" is your will and the life review determines the outcome, so be it. You experience what you were determined to experience.

All this information is not new. It was, is and always will be available. Most people are determined not to listen to their own conscience, for this is where the information, the knowing, is. Hence all the separate heavens with masses of spirits waiting to meet their own particular or peculiar vision of god, in their own vision of heaven, complete with pecking order of holiness and piety, in-fighting, argument and debate (there is no violence outside of the earth experience). This is the realm of partial awareness.

In all existence or experience of reality outside the earth, manifestation is instantaneous and you have what you want or will. You are aware of the law of abundance and want for nothing. All your needs will be met. You experience what you will until you choose not to. That is, you can stay or exist here in the illusion of your choice for as long as you want.

There is one exception - the realm of unawareness. This is where some choose to experience because of their belief system. Insistence on crime and punishment, vengeance and retribution, sin and penance. When they view their thoughts, words and actions from an aware point, their insistence or belief system comes back to them ("what you give, so shall you receive"). They send themselves to hell. This is a free will choice (as is a visit to the lords of karma) even when they are aware or are made aware of the pointlessness with regard to their spiritual growth. No other will try to stop them for to do so would be a violation of their free will and unconditional love could not do this.

A soul aspect can also move towards full awareness if it chooses to through experiencing love for itself and all others. As soon as the thought arises, your guides and angel (who stay with you until you reach a level of awareness) arrange for the right circumstances for you to become aware of how you behave and react and its effects on your spiritual growth. You can enrol in schools of healing, practice towards enlightenment including song, dance, music, meditation, laughter, play, creative art and talks or teachings. You will become aware of your over-soul and of any aspects it has incarnated on earth. You can work towards full awareness by helping, through sending or transmuting loving thoughts to guide these aspects, as well as others who are about to incarnate, that request guides. You will work in groups within bigger groups not unlike ripples in a pond, circles within circles, guiding spirits on earth and guiding spirits in the realm of unawareness in the spirit world.

To reincarnate in order to become aware or undo what has been done, is in itself an unaware action, thought and feeling. To feel you have to do anything is an unaware thought. For simply to feel love is all that is required. A heart full of love while human or being full of love in the case of spirit, has no room for fear i.e. guilt, regret or any other negative energies. Reincarnation mostly happens from the state of partial awareness with spirits working to their own agenda. It is not right or wrong, it is simply unnecessary. Others, who choose to reincarnate, do so as light workers. They come from a level of awareness or even full awareness, in order to bring their love and knowing to others or all on earth, with the intention of trying to shorten the needless pain and suffering born of fear on earth. Many of these will spend part of their lives suffering themselves, for they too will forget. But the detailed arrangements made before birth ensures, through their guides, that they find their chosen path or task. It falls into place and they know it when it is presented to them. Others will also know of them. They will be drawn (guided) to them or the message they bring. Their enegy will be of love and they will bring healing, comfort, understanding, knowing and awareness by their presence, their talks and teachings and sometimes their silence, their writings, paintings, inventions, organisations and foundations. These are bearers of the light. They carry the seeds of change. They are no different to any other. They are not more or less special than any other, simply more aware. They remembered who and what they and you really are – an expression of divine love.

This is what you can and will take with you. Sooner or later, the choice is yours. There is no death, only fear of it. As you face your smaller fears in life, the changes and challenges of new situations and circumstances that the earth experience is, you will realise the fear was not as powerful as you expected. From learning to drive or swim, meeting people, starting something new or ending something old. To bungi – jumping, stopping smoking, drinking alcohol and other drugs or getting a divorce.

After people here on earth face the fear of change, they often wonder why they did not do it sooner. It is the release of fear that brings this feeling. It is called success and is very often hijacked by the ego – self and can get lost in the illusion. Success is a feeling, not an image. You cannot bring your image of success (that what you have been showing to the world) with you. But you can bring the feeling, if you have it. Bring love and joy into your life from within and you will feel success forever, for you will have succeeded. This is full awareness.
Blessings to all.

About the angel of the Lord who appeared unto Mary. No, I was not responsible. That was a human birth, conceived in the normal way. Yes, Mary did see me and recognised me, for we are old friends and she became aware of her life path and that of her first – born child. This event is still happening today and will go on happening. Many parents are aware of their child's potential to bring peace and love to the world. These parents create a peaceful and loving environment and teach by example. The message of the Christ child Jesus is carried in every child. For every child is the Christ child with a different name. His message was simple. One persons love can reach millions. This is true of others known as prophets and it is also true of you. Your love can reach millions on earth and in spirit. Reach in to find it and let it pour from your very being. There are billions upon billions who long for it and even more billions upon billions who long to help to pour their love through you. There is nothing or nobody unworthy of unconditional love, least the earth itself. We in spirit, at the level of full awareness, ask that you on earth respect its' wonders, it's beauty and bounty. It is for all to share. We urge you to learn to love. Not to give or receive love, to live love. To feel you are love and all around you is made of love. This is full awareness.

LEVELS OF AWARENESS

There are eight levels of awareness:

1st.   Non – awareness, known as hell, the underworld.
2nd.   Partial awareness.
3rd.   Awareness.
4th.   Service to awareness.
5th.   Purification.
6th.   Awareness.
7th.   Service to full awareness.
8th.   Full awareness, oneness.

These levels or plains are not locations as on earth, they are states of being. A human can evolve through all these levels without physically moving from one place to another or one lifetime to another. Examples are some Tibetan and Indian masters. Although withdrawing from the outside world in its physical form into monasteries in remote locations is not necessary, this too serves its own purpose for those who enter them. All humans, including the masters and incarnated angels, move from one state of being to another as a matter of fact. It is part of the process of life, the ups and downs, the highs and lows, experienced on a daily basis, within the day on an hourly basis, within the hour on a moment to moment basis. Mood swings and roundabouts, our sense of being or the humour we are in, keeps on changing in response to our outer and our inner circumstances. This is where our own levels of awareness come into play. As above, so below. We can and do choose at which level we respond, act, react or exist on.

FIRST LEVEL

To respond or exist at a level of unawareness is to be your own worst enemy e.g. to hold fear, anger and hate for yourself (and so hurt yourself) and see this in others and so judge them, unaware of your own and others spiritual nature. At this level, people allow themselves to be used, abused, manipulated, controlled and killed. Or they themselves do the using and abusing, manipulating, controlling and killing. This, in both the spiritual and physical world (earth), is called the underworld or hell. It is hell for those who dwell or are drawn into it and for those who are (or allow themselves to be) affected by the thoughts, words and actions of unaware spirits and people. Every unaware thought, word and action is simply that - unaware.

SECOND LEVEL

To respond or exist at a level of partial awareness is to see others as your worst enemy or at least a threat to your existence and to be self – conscious, self – righteous, imposing, dictating, ruthless and superior (holier than thou). To be partially aware of some sort of spirituality, although limited to your own point of view or opinion.

"God is on my side not yours", "I am right, you are wrong", "I am good, you are bad", "My way is the only way" and to be so convinced by yourself or others, cause your thoughts, words and actions to lead you into and out of the level of unawareness. Just as a person at levels of unawareness can rise to the level of partial awareness. For most people, this is as far as they go during a lifetime, moving between these two states of being; the ups and downs and the highs and lows. Levels of awareness do not exist side by side as rich neighbourhood/ poor neighbourhood, or first, second or third world countries, but as energy levels or clouds of consciousness (thought form) that souls tune into and attract to themselves (like to like) and which they emanate. Most of this energy is negative (which simply means not positive) in both the highs and lows. Pity, greed, bitterness, jealousy, possessiveness, ignorance, pretence, resignation and elitism. In fact every other word, thought or action that is not pure unconditional love is within the first two levels or states of being. This includes the highs that are short lived as you soon seek another high and another and another. This is sexual pleasure, lust, money, drugs, alcohol, image and attention, again without love. Partial awareness is simply that – partial awareness.

THIRD LEVEL

To respond or exist at a level of awareness is to see no
enemies. You only see unaware or partially aware thoughts,
words and actions in yourself as you choose how you
respond or react to your inner and your outer
circumstances. On this level you find harmony and balance
through the ups and downs. You are aware of your spiritual
nature and that of others. You learn about your feelings
and your own responsibility to those feelings. You work
through to your inner child and conditioning. This is the
level of self healing and healing others. You open up to
guidance that will be presented to you in many ways e.g.
television, books, seemingly chance meetings!, newspaper
articles/ advertisements, psychic healers/ teachers or
directly from guides and angels. On earth, some become
aware through near death experiences or someone else's
passing touches them. The energy here is mostly love, with
any other energy entering briefly for you to notice, become
aware of and adjust your response. You cannot hide or
pretend. You will become aware of your reality and how
you feel from moment to moment. This is awareness.

FOURTH LEVEL

Service to awareness is simply spreading your love (in
whatever form that may take) from a position of
awareness. It is a natural progression from the level of
awareness. When a spirit becomes aware, it cannot help but

share. This is its true nature. It will not have its own limited or self interest at heart but that of the purest and highest good of all, which is love. These spirits are the readers of the soul, the guides, the teachers, the healers, shamans, mystics, the adventurers, the peacemakers and the community builders. They are truly leaders. They are leading the multitude back to awareness. This process is happening at an ever- quickening rate and will continue to do so. Spirit who exist or live at this level transmute fear in all its manifestations, by the power of their love and the knowing that they/ we are of divine nature.

FIFTH LEVEL

Purification is the process leading to full awareness. At this level, a spirit is aware of its own part in the bigger scheme of things. It is aware of past lives and any issues left unresolved are worked on and released. No separation exists at this level of awareness. Love for all is at the heart of a spirit that is purifying. Non- judgement and endless compassion are tools or thoughts which energise and start the process of purification ("there by the grace of god go I"), which not only impacts or effects the spirit or person but it impacts or effects all. As one purifies, so do all. The earth itself is at this level of existence and works in unity with those in spirit and in physical form. As we purify ourselves, we purify the earth. As the earth purifies itself, it purifies us. This process is also quickening up and will continue to do so.

SIXTH LEVEL

Awareness after purification is the level of existence of teachers, masters and healers. These come in many forms and guises, known and unknown, seen and unseen. The energy at this level is unconditional love and dispassion. The spirit or person has attained freedom or enlightenment from all past life experiences and exists in the moment. On earth, this can be something of a struggle. Because of the perception of time (past, present and future), it is impossible for humans to exist here constantly, but to return to the moment as soon as you become aware of its absence. That is when you are in your head, in your past or future or someone else's past or future – unnecessary mind babble. It is necessary to leave the moment in order to plan ahead or retrieve the past, in order to heal. To return and keep returning to the moment is the best that can be achieved. When humans exist in the moment they add their energy to that moment which is the one and only thing that exists. It is commonly shared by all six billion plus humans. The moment and time are not one and the same. The moment is not a measure of time. Time is an invention of the mind. The moment is conception, creation, birth, continuous existence. There is no death. This is awareness after purification.

SEVENTH LEVEL

Service to full awareness may best be described as vocation or dedication to the light. Spirits, incarnate or not, with and without a body, whose sole purpose is the spreading of the word, the light and the way. These spirits are the messengers. The energy here is divine energy. Undiluted by the mind and its' illusions and delusions, but focused on and by the mind. These spirits are the workers of miracles. Fully aware that each and every moment and all that is contained in that moment, is a miracle, the miracle of life. When we tune into the divine energy contained in the moment, we live the miracle. We are the miracle and therefore create miracles with our words, thoughts and actions. This is what a true martyr is. A spirit that lovingly and freely emanates its life and light for the good of all. It is not sacrificing your life for your own goal or that of any one group (which would be an unaware action and thought form). The word "martyr" is only used to put a context on an existence and has no relevance outside of that.

EIGHTH LEVEL

Full awareness is the level of oneness. The energy here is pure, unconditional love, simple and uncomplicated. There is no more to be asked or answered. It is a state of being. This, you, all of you, all of us, will achieve. For "thy will, your will, our will, be done on earth as it is in heaven".

SEEK

Inside there's a spirit
with a different point of view.
Take the time to listen
It will guide the way for you.

It will not judge or label you
pure compassion without end.
It helps you learn from your mistakes
It has always been your friend.

It's been with you since you started
from the moment you chose life.
It will show the way when you get lost
As you journey back to light.

Inside there is a spirit
pure love, unconditional, for you.
Go inside, embrace it, that's all you have to do.
It will help you learn to love again
first yourself, then others too.

If you feel you can't go in
that you may not have the strength
you're scared or pride won't let you
then just turn around to a friend.

Reach out your hand to the out reached
hands of those who will show you what to do
and you can see and live life differently
from your spirits point of view.

CHAPTER ELEVEN

GUILT AND FORGIVENESS

Guilt is one of the most powerful energies on earth. It is dense and has a heavy vibration (it weighs heavy on us). It is born out of fear and it is fed on and thrives on the negative thought forms that we have about ourselves.

Forgiveness melts and transforms guilt. Guilt replaces responsibility. It says "I didn't choose to" and we cover it up with excuses. We allow ourselves to think, feel and act in a cycle of experiences that bring opportunity for us to take responsibility and control our thoughts, feelings and actions. This cycle can last a lifetime if you allow it and it is easy to allow this to happen. It is also easy not to allow this to happen, to take responsibility.

How to do this? Make a list and focus on one issue at a time. Have a look at the things in your life that make you feel guilty or that you feel guilty about. Things you have said or done or haven't said or done in the past. The things you think about or don't think about. The rules and regulations you have or have not been following. Ask yourself who, why and when?

WHO?

Who has me thinking like this?
(No one can control your thoughts).

Who has me feeling like this?
(No one can control your feelings).

Who has me acting like this?
(No one can control your actions).
You have total control, you choose.

WHY?

Why am I thinking this way about this?
Why am I feeling this way about this?
Why am I acting this way about this?

WHEN?

Look to where the thinking or thought process started.
How long have you felt like this about the issue? Do you
still want to feel the same now? Choose to keep it or
change it. If you choose change, learn from it and thank it
for the lesson and forgive.

Look to where the feeling started. How long have you felt
like this about this issue? Do you still want to feel the same
now? Choose to keep it or change it. Learn, thank it and
forgive.

Look to where the action or behaviour patterns started. How long have you been acting or behaving like this? Choose to keep it or change, learn, thank and forgive.

The choice is always yours in the now. Blaming others, the past or circumstances is not taking responsibility, in the now. We allow ourselves the choice.

Forgiveness is not about forgetting or letting go of things that you are hurting from. It is not forgetting about things that caused you harm or pretending it never happened, ignoring it and getting on with it. Forgiving is a divine energy. It is love, love is forgiving. You must have a thing before you can give it or the experience of it, to others. You must forgive yourself first. Know forgiveness for yourself and then you will know forgiveness for others. If you cannot forgive another, you cannot forgive yourself. Forgive yourself for holding on to hurt or anger. Forgive yourself for thinking, feeling and acting on negative thought forms or ideas of how it should or could be, or was.

Forgive yourself for not forgiving yourself.
Change, learn, thank and forgive.
The choice is always yours. Always only in the now.

CONNECT

See the beauty in the ugliness,
see the light behind your eye.
A diversity of wonders,
within a multitude of colours in a sky.

Why does one tiny bird stay?
When the rest of the flock flies away?
How does it feel
when you live life as a meal?
Every hour,
Every day,
You are prey.

What is it that makes a seed pop?
No longer a shell,
dividing and multiplying into life.
Internal forces growing within.
External forces we cannot comprehend.
The first seed,
first raindrop,
first light.
Limited thinking and timing.
We must have beginning and end.

We face the four points of a compass.
Symmetrically divided the globe.

We fight over invisible lines of a map.
Our children are bought
and are sold by our children.
Held for ransom by mothers and fathers.
We collectively abandon our old.

Abortions and birth.
New life,
new death.
We kill killers
and hold up our heads.
Human rights.
Human wrongs.
All side by side,
there's nothing wrong.
As we point our finger in moral attack,
we ignore the three fingers,
pointing back.

A material world of illusions,
manifested to make us look grand.
Distractions from global confusion,
grabbing and hoarding as much as we can.
While we walk the thin line
between need and greed,
half the world starves,
while half the world feeds,
On power,
awards,
medals,
pedestals,

votes,
fortune,
fame.
Behind these great illusions,
born naked,
we are all the same dying,
In a short space of time.

See the beauty.
Connect.
Feel.
Start enjoying.

ONENESS AND SEPARATION

God is the creator. He/ she/ it has many names and titles. Every he, every she, every it that ever was, is now and ever shall be. That is god. He is still creating now, at this moment, in me, with you, through us. We are God. God is us. You, them, that and me.

God is all things and more. Visible and invisible. God is not a separate entity or king or supreme being that talks from the sky, unless you choose it to. God is not in me more than you, him more than her, this more than that, unless you choose it to be.

Your choice creates your reality. You choose it to be, so be it. This is the power of God. This is unconditional love. Love without restrictions, limits, boundaries, rules, regulations, judgement, opinions, punishment, condemnation and separation.

We have, all of us as individuals, a God given choice, free will, to experience what we will. Thy will be done on earth. Thy will is your will. We are all, everything is, a part of God. This is oneness. All part of the one. Free will is not confined to the earth experience, limited by physical boundaries and time. Free will is God, love, limitless and so it is with you/ me/ us. Free will does not start when you become an adult or abandoned child. Free will always was, is now and ever will be. And so it is a free will choice to live a lifetime or lifetimes on earth.

This is when we choose to separate from the oneness of God and all. We move from the higher vibration of spirit being, without the physical restriction, into an environment of dense vibration of matter and gravity.

Being born into the earth experience was and is choice. You choose (even design) your body. Where, when and to what parents (with their permission), in what country, conditions and circumstances. Most bodies function the same: physical body, emotional body, mental body – everybody functions the same, yet separately. We choose the illusion of separation from the oneness. This is when we forget who and what we are. We choose separation in order to choose not to be separate. We love "love", we love the oneness and we love to find or remember our oneness on earth. This is heaven on earth – oneness as a state of being, "do unto others as you would have others do unto you". For we are all one. What you do to, for or against another, you do to, for or against all and yourself. For what you give, so shall you receive. This is unconditional love, love and oneness.

Separation. The illusion of separation. The umbilical cord is cut. The baby's' first cry. A new world, strange for the spirit who has chosen to forget. Our first experience is of a feeling of separation, abandonment, aloneness. The being is born into a world where separation and the feeling of it is reinforced by its' skin colour, physical shape, country of origin, parents' religious beliefs and cultural barriers, economic value, educational and occupational limits, laws and borders. All are reinforced as the child grows,

123

experiences and learns. The child uses these experiences to form its' own perceptions of life and how the world, its' world, works. It too works within these boundaries. This is conditioning, learnt behaviour. As the child grows into and through adulthood, it chooses to live within or challenge and push out/ breakdown the barriers and boundaries.

This is free will. Throughout this period, the first feeling, our first experience, returns time and time again. The one of separation, abandonment and aloneness. No matter how much love, affection or attention we give or receive and sometimes no matter what we do, the feeling still comes back, again and again. And so it will, until you choose it not to. Until you see through the illusion of separation; until you return to the oneness. When you become aware of this, you start to heal.

INTERNAL UNIVERSE

I have an inner sense of knowing.
Absolutely nothing to do with anything I have ever learned
or been taught.
It is not knowledge.
It is knowing a feeling of it.
I trust this inner-sense with and for my very life.
And I am grateful, eternally grateful.
For without it I would be in a very dark place.
Where worries and anguish and pain dwell.
When sometimes shadows from the darkness cast
themselves over me.
It is into this inner knowledge I go
for support, substance, guidance, peace and love.
And I know there is not a power or energy that can stop
me entering,
except my own thoughts.
So I use my knowing as a weapon against these with a
mantra.

A MANTRA

In me.
With me.
Through me.
This is what I do.
I offer the divine love in me,
to the divine love inside of you.
Close your eyes and know,
I am loved
and it is so.
Open up your heart and mind.
Release your fear and you will find,
a warm embrace,
a welcome smile.
Stay and visit for a while.
Come in again at any time.
It may not happen your first time.
It will not happen if you don't try.
To help clear your thoughts, repeat these lines:
In me.
With me.
Through me.
You are loved.
Love is divine.

CUTTING THE TIES

During the lifetime of any spirit, it forms many bonds or ties with others. These are spiritual bonds or agreements made before incarnation. The strongest of these ties will be with our earth mother, then our father and siblings. Where others have replaced these figures, bonds or ties will form with those significant others. The agreement is basically to take care of our needs until such time as we can meet our own needs; to be our caretakers not our owners.

These ties are like tiny threads connecting us. As they are of a spiritual nature or faster vibration, we cannot see or touch them. Yet we can pass feelings through them. Time or distance does not matter with these threads. They will exist until recognised and cut with love and forgiveness. Cutting them without love and forgiveness will reinforce or strengthen them. There is a physical need to cut these ties when we reach a certain age or state of being in order to move into adulthood.

Many cultures and tribal traditions have a ceremony or rite of passage, where young men and women go through a ritualised initiation into adulthood. This is a collective or communal cutting of the ties, letting them go into the world, as they will. In many more cultures and tribal traditions, these practices have long since been abandoned. With community support systems gone, the family must stick together to survive. Here, the cutting of the ties is not recognised or acknowledged. It is seen as a rejection of the family principles, the rules and regulations, religious and cultural habits. These will be represented by the parents as principles in the family and be seen as a rejection of them, also. This belief system is based on fear. It is a communal or collective belief of lack, not enough to go around, or for all, storing and hoarding, taking possession of people and things. This does not stop the ties forming or remaining. In fact, we form even more ties and bonds with our material possessions. These ties restrict our spiritual growth, limiting our experience to that of our parents and grandparents. The ties connect to our emotional self or centre, hence to our inner-child and all our early experiences. It is through these that we pass on our own belief system, our behaviour and emotional patterns.

Spiritually, we all have to face the cutting of the ties. Physically, it will come at some point in a lifetime. We all must part from our loved ones who remain on earth at the leaving or death of the body. It is easier for the spirit to accept its' new state of being and move to the world of spirit if the ties have been cut earlier in that lifetime. There are opportunities in the spirit world to cut the ties for those who choose to do so. The ties represent a spirits' connection to the earth experience, not unlike plugging into an energy grid. As long as you remain plugged in, you cannot move on. The cutting of the ties can be likened to unplugging or disconnecting. When this is done while you are in physical form, you free yourself to experience what you will, without restriction or need for approval or recognition. You no longer feel guilt or anxiety for being who you are, without the need to be accepted by those you are tied to. You also free them to be who they are and accept it as is, without the need for them to change.

All this needs to be experienced from a position of love, unconditional love of self. This is the tool to cut away the ties. You must find it for yourself before you can know it and use it as a tool. Through meditation and working with your inner-child, you can find unconditional love. In meditation, visualise the person or thing you wish to cut the ties with. If it is a person, you will be connecting with their higher or spirit self. If you need to express feelings or thoughts or explain actions, this is a safe place to do it. You can talk to them, you may sense a response. They may even talk back. If you need to forgive, or seek forgiveness, do it with love. Forgive yourself, visualise a thread between you, connecting the two of you. Sometimes this may take the form of chains or ropes, barbed wire or daisy chains. Whatever they appear as, visualise an appropriate tool to cut, hack, saw or snip the connections and affirm to yourself and the other person that any ties that now form will be only of light.

Ask your guardian angel to assist you. You don't have to sense or feel the angel. You don't even have to believe in angels if you are doing this from your heart. Your angel will know you are ready. This is part of their job. They will not get too involved with your life unless you ask (except if you are in danger of passing over before your time) as they have utter respect for your free will.

ALONE AMONG FRIENDS

Cut the ties little boys, cut the ties.
Cut the ties little girls as well.
Free yourself,
be yourself.
Answer to thee thyself.
Cut the ties and you will heal.

Cut the ties from a mother,
allow her to learn who she is.
Cut the ties from a father,
allow him return to within.

Cut the ties little boys in grown up men,
who expect to be mothered all over again.
Cut the ties little girls who are women now,
stop pretending. Playtime is over.

Cut the ties that stir the pain inside,
as you revert from adult into child.
Full of expectations and unfulfilled dreams.
Disappointed with reality, all is as it seems.
Cut the ties.

Cut the ties that form a knot in your gut,
that tightens each time you feel hurt, ignored, neglected,
exposed.

Cut the ties. Take control
and those feelings will go.

Cut the ties which form judgement on others,
untangle yourself from the pack.
Cut the ties from your sisters.
Cut the ties from your brothers.
Allow them to find their own path.

Cut the ties of self – imposed limits.
The ties that are holding you back.
Turn yourself from possession into person,
unique, individual, courageous and certain.
Cut the ties from the past and relax in the now. Relax.
Cut the ties from your sons and your daughters,
they have their own lessons to learn.
Your truth to yourself, a lesson for you,
your freedom a lesson for them.
Cut the ties.

Cut the ties that bind you with guilt to the rules,
you choose to do what you're told.
Be good and don't upset elders.
You choose elders' upsets as yours.
Cut the tie that links choose into "have to",
"must do" what others expect.
Cut the ties that reach outwards for notice,
reach in, you'll find self-respect.

Heal the ties that you cut,
with love for yourself.

Heal the ties that you cut,
with your truth.
Acknowledge your return to me myself
and see myself,
again.
You live all alone among friends.

BAGGAGE

It is what we carry or have others carry for us in our relationships with life. It is all that we experience in our childhood and conditioning, which we bring into all our relationships. That is, all relationships including the one we have with ourself or selves. Yes, I did say selves because we all have very different personalities that do not show themselves to all people at all times. They are held behind the persona or personality; the face we show to the world when we are holding ourselves together. Restricting how we behave or carry ourselves in public or in the company of loved ones to the persona that is expected of us. The way in which the side of us we are showing interacts and reacts with another or others is all about control. Not only controlling who and what side we show, inside or out, but also controlling or trying to control those around us. This may be better understood with a scenario or picture built up around it.

A man is dressing in his room. He looks into the mirror to see what he looks like. He decides he is dressed appropriately. His outside persona is acceptable; not to himself, he would much rather wear his jeans and worn, old boots. Then he talks to himself or rather, to his reflection. "You'll do ok. Just relax and smile. Don't loose the head. It will be over in a few hours. You have to show up, you can't miss this. Smile and get it over and done with".

He was going to a family celebration that he would rather not be going to. Not that he had a more pressing or important (to him) place to be or things to do, he just didn't like all the pretence around family celebrations. He knew some or most of the personalities behind the personality front of the members of his family. It was on this perception that he judged them, so he went to the celebration. He smiled and told all who asked that he was fine. Behind the smile, a different personality was connecting with his brain other than the one smiling outwardly. He was angry within himself. The part of him that most wanted to express itself, was held back behind a façade of fear. So, on with the party.

After a few drinks, the inner personality builds courage to burst out in anger as the outer-self loses control. He tells his family what he thinks of their party of pretence and storms out in a rage, which builds up the more he thinks about his family. He now feels victimised and his anger turns inward. Another personality has emerged, over-shadowing the angry one, which now retreats. His feelings only aired for a short time. The anger retreats inwardly with him. Now the victim-self is in control and he believes that he is not in control. Nothing is his fault. Others make him feel this way. He wants to cry. His spirit-self cries and the un-shed tears become bitter. His unspoken feelings, emotions and thoughts are swallowed and stored again, as they have been doing all his life. He falls asleep under a cloud of self-pity that night.

The next morning he would rather forget about last night. As his friends, guilt and remorse, face into the day ahead, ready to remind him of his actions, words and feelings, bombarding him with flashbacks. This time everything is his fault. He upset the party. He didn't want to go in the first place. The circle is complete. He is back to where he started.

As he shaves for work, he thinks to himself "I'd love to grow a beard". As he tightened his necktie, he thinks, "I'd love to dress more casually". He shrugs his shoulders with a sigh of resignation and goes out to work. This man is angry with himself. The pretence he sees in others, is his own pretence. His anger is his fear of change. Fear of speaking his feelings, thoughts and emotions. To stop the pretence and be and do what he wants.

The baggage this man is carrying is his own. All the different personalities are him. All the attack and defence mechanisms are his. It is inevitable that he will continue to carry this baggage with him until he chooses to unload, unburden, let go and lighten his load.

This scenario is only a means of getting a concept across. The details can be changed to suit most people. The object was to show, in a mirrored way, what we know already. We have many faces behind the mask.
The way to unload this baggage is simple but it is not easy. Fear will be encountered, faced and experienced. Under the heading "fear", is a whole array of twisted thought forms, emotions and feelings stretching back to our earliest

moments and back to past lives for some. It takes courage and bravery to choose to do this rather than have it forced upon us and having to change when circumstances become intolerable. Whenever a person chooses to do this, the first step is always inward. It is the start of an inner-journey into spirit. Through all of the mish-mash, the maze of issues, to a quiet and safe refuge, a healing centre within. This baggage is your thought process and behaviour patterns. The case must be opened for examination and the contents claimed, labelled, stored or discarded. They must be acknowledged as yours. No matter how they came to you in the first place, they are now in your possession. You are carrying them as baggage and they are affecting you and those close to you. This will happen until you stop, rest and get to know and care for and love all of yourself. Allow all of your personalities to express themselves in a caring and gentle way.

Responsibility must be accepted and practised. In cases where we say something came and took over, we can learn to sense that something and recognise it before it takes over and the situations where it is likely to occur. This way, we can choose to control how we act or whether we react in the old pattern. When we choose to be in control, we no longer blame others for our feelings so we no longer feel others are controlling us and we no longer wish to control others. We allow them control of their own lives, even if we perceive their lives to be out of control, we no longer judge. We can see unclaimed baggage and understand.

We have changed our perception and no longer allow how we used to perceive life to control us. This means being in charge of all our personalities and their different needs. This all takes time, a lifetime or lifetimes. It is a process we must go through or live through.

This baggage belongs to the earth experience and you cannot take it with you into the spirit world. Its' vibrations are too heavy, so you must learn or re-learn, educate or un-educate, all the different personalities smothering the spirit within. The spirit that is crying for release. Crying to express itself with love and joy and gratitude, to be free to speak its' truth, to walk its' chosen path (unrestricted by constraints of fear and guilt); to be light hearted and free – free to move into the world of spirit without earthly baggage.

INNER-CHILD

Our inner-child is a most beautiful gift, for the child in us all holds a memory deep within, of our connection to spirit. All the infants' memories are held within our aura. We as grown – ups, do not have to remember these experiences. In most cases we don't, but sometimes deep inside ourselves, we remember or know. The inner – child holds our key to freedom. The key to freeing our spirit from the cycle of death, life, death, life or reincarnation and the balancing forces of karma. So we must connect with our inner – child during an incarnation or earth lifetime. The child holds the key to the baggage trunk!

All our thoughts, feelings and actions relate to the child; the fear and feeling of being unloved, alone, abandoned and all the experiences the child has learned as it grows. It takes on the patterns or characteristics, consciously or unconsciously, of its' surroundings. Not just the people who care, nurture, feed and clothe but also the atmosphere in which this is carried out. A child's thought process has not begun to develop so it uses all its' senses to feel its' new environment. It can sense fear or love, anger or joy, acceptance or rejection. It can sense tension or happiness in the space it occupies, while it may not be aware of who or what is causing it to feel like this. It remembers the feelings and uses these as a basis or foundation on which all other experiences are built upon and related to as the child grows.

As our thought process develops, we are taught how to behave and what is acceptable to show and what we must not show. This is the start of our multi – personality developing inside. Because of a lack of outer expression we learn to conform in order to please, to feel loved and accepted and in some cases not to be hurt, slapped or punished.

The circumstances we are born into are not coincidences. They are the perfect conditions, for the spirit, who manifested itself as that child, has chosen them to experience all of this. To live through a turmoil of emotions, feelings, thoughts and expression and yet find peace, freedom and love for itself and those around it. Some adults feel like they want to cry if shouted at or if they feel they are being verbally abused. To cry would show the other that they are causing another to feel hurt. Learned behaviour dictates how we react. In this case we can withdraw and take it, shout abuse back or strike out in anger. Whatever the reaction, it will stem back to childhood.

Observe a couple, two people in a relationship who have not worked through their inner – child issues. They act and react the same scenario over and over again; falling in and out of what they perceive as love. Not talking, sulking, sending silent signals and expecting the other to pick these up and behave or act as they are expecting the other to act. With both parties engaged in this process, mirroring to each other what they fail to see in themselves or their perception of how it should be, both have carried their own baggage into this relationship and will pass it on to any children they may raise together.

This makes the child's journey towards enlightenment just as difficult and traumatic or dramatic as yours but there is always divine intervention (a short cut to enlightenment). If you become enlightened on your journey you also pass this experience on to your children or children in your care. This enables them to live a life of joy and abundance from an early age and so they will spread their love and pass it on to their children or children in their care.

The old patterns of fear and guilt have formed chains that bind you into family traditions, cultural, religious, political and philosophical belief systems, each forming a link in the chain. Some of these beliefs date back hundreds or thousands of years. These belong to your soul group or spirit family; a group of individual entities who work together as one, towards a common goal. You are forming another link in this chain. You are representing all that has gone before down through these links. With each lifetime of any of your soul group, there is a chance to break these patterns. A chance to stop the loop, break the chain and build a ladder of light. When you become enlightened, your entire soul group benefits. If you do not, all your soul group learns by what we label "mistakes", which in fact are our teachers. We learn by our mistakes. We experience a thing repeatedly until we learn. We choose to keep the experience or change it to experience something else.

We experience what we perceive. If you perceive life to be a burden, full of suffering, injustice and something that must be endured, so be it – that is what you will experience. If you perceive life to be boring, pointless and mundane, so be it – that is what you will experience. If you perceive life as violent, full of hate, judgement, fear and vengeance, so be it – these are what you will experience. If you perceive life as loving, joyous and full of wonderful things, so be it. The child born into conflict situations so much wants to bring change, but through conditioning almost always gets enmeshed and embroiled into the conflict itself. Be this a small scale family conflict or larger community or national conflict. So the first step in the process of healing the inner – child is to withdraw from conflict situations. That is, not to lie down and accept the situation. It means accepting the situation and standing up. Acknowledge it as it is without being enmeshed in it, without it affecting who you are and not reacting to it while seeing it for what it is – old patterns. So look at the patterns of the child in you; how you react in different situations with different people. See it from another perspective. See it from the child perspective. Also understand why the child feels this way and reacts this way. Then change the perception to that of awareness. Recognise the difference between the old feelings and your new perception of them. Then take control of your actions, thoughts and feelings.

Knowing this process takes time. Be gentle on yourself. Nurture and love the inner – child. Understand it in others.

The process often involves breaking what has been perceived from the child experience as rules, must do's and don'ts. Living up to expected standards and moral codes of conduct. This is just within the family! For this is where our inner – child takes centre stage, performing within boundaries where you may feel upset but don't do or say anything to upset. The boundaries only exist in your mind. In reality, a stranger may come into the same situation and say and do as he or she pleases without fear. Those that you are so fearful of upsetting, accept the stranger as he or she is. They may judge and form an opinion. This will not have an effect on the stranger, who could be a friend or neighbour, because they were not conditioned by these people and so any controlling signals will not register. Therefore there will be no triggering of the thoughts, feelings and actions of the child. This would not be the same for the stranger in their own family, unless they are aware of and have worked through their inner – child issues.

If we go back to our scenario (see baggage), although the man (physically he looked like a man, inside he felt like a child), did not want to go to the celebration, he went, fearful of upsetting his mother which in turn would upset his father and siblings. "Don't upset mother" was what the family's belief system was based upon. His mother held the power. Her inner – child was so strong and powerful that her fear of being unloved caused her to take both her husband and her children's power. His father was of the same belief system and was torn between not upsetting his own mother and his wife. He was powerless. Both his grandparents and parents had passed this belief system on. He could see the pattern in his siblings and their children. He could also see the angry side of them. Like him, they all had their outbursts. Angry at their loss of power and feelings of helplessness, embedded in their collective belief system is the notion that when mother is upset, love is withdrawn and whomever upset mother may cause love to be withdrawn from all. Sides are therefore taken. Judgement and anger are sent towards the perpetrator, intensifying their feeling of isolation and abandonment. This has been the pattern or cycle in this mans' life, his learned behaviour.

This is only one scenario. Father, brother, sister, son and daughter can all replace the mother as the power figure. In some or most cases it is a constant power struggle, with the power switching from the father to the mother, mother to daughter, father to son and brother to sister. These struggles can be sublime or obvious, like the pecking order in a roost of chickens.

Our child has protection. Our ego, pride and dignity build a barrier of self – esteem that the child hides behind. Sometimes this barrier is used as a weapon. In the case of a bully, the child is so fearful of showing how they really feel inside that this barrier hardens, not letting feelings in or out. When barriers between two people harden, communication is almost impossible until one becomes aware of this and relents, softens and drops the barrier.

This also happens on a collective scale. Hence wars and peace. The person or collective, i.e. country, who has learned through becoming aware of the inner – child (past experiences), find their own power and no longer gives it away or seeks to take it from another and so becomes detached. This is breaking the chains. It is also the start of new patterns forming. You should be aware of this as it can be a time of confusion, where there is an urge to retreat to the perceived safety of what you know best, the old patterns. This is, in a sense, growing – up. Others, still caught in (or who have chosen to stay in) the old patterns will not encourage or maybe understand the changes you are making and going through. It is an inner journey you can only make alone. Expectations play a huge part with our inner – child. From a very early age we form our own picture. Our very own view of our very own world. We fill up this picture with the things we like or would like, real or imagined. If we experience love, affection or attention, this is the basis of the picture. If there was little of these, the picture will be based on the need for these. As the child grows and learns, it builds up a complete picture, all in the mind, of how they want it to be. Sometimes down to the minute details i.e. the partner, the job, the house, children and family. All of these will be in there. This is how we co - create – by our thoughts.

We hold a picture or idea in our mind and focus our time and energy towards that picture. We create our reality as we work towards that picture. The picture works towards us. Work is necessary, so is action. The picture is also a belief system. The belief is that when the picture is complete, everything will be right and that we will have happiness and love. This is what is expected. People will have a role to play in our picture, even before we meet them or even before they are born!

All this is based on the expectation that love enters our life at some stage and makes us happy. Material things add to this making a statement to the world (or your world) that "I have achieved". We expect happy ever after. Happy ever after is possible when partners share the same picture, but expectations are seldom spoken about to our partners. The fact that we expect it means we feel we do not have to or should not have to, ask or talk to our partner or family member. It is when the reality we have created does not fit the picture that our behaviour/ emotional patterns emerge. We may have all the material things and more than we wanted, or not, but when people/ things/ achievements do not live or perform up to our expectations, our happiness with all our perceived achievements is short lived. Our bubble bursts and we feel disappointment. This is when our inner – child takes control and the disappointment will trigger an emotional response, an old one. We feel lonely, rejected, abandoned and unloved, even unlovable. Our pride or ego is hurt! This triggers our behaviour patters of sulking, temper outbursts, silence, attack or withdrawal. We all have our own patterns. This is usually the underlying reason for power struggles within relationships and family. Whose picture are we in? Whose expectations and standards are to be met and lived up to? This is when adults act like children. Un-responsible for their own feelings, thoughts and actions. We blame who or whatever disappointed us. These disappointments can form part of an overall pattern (the ups and downs in life), until someone shouts stop. The shout to stop must be aimed at you, at your inner – child.

The shout, a cry – out for change, must come from the adult in control or with a willingness to be in control. You do not necessarily have to know what you want, only what you do not want to experience any more. This is the start of taking responsibility for you. Shouting stop at others is putting your expectations onto them. You must take responsibility for your own feelings and thoughts and actions. No more blaming others or situations – no more allowing our disappointments to trigger off un – responsible reactions. "Responsibility" is your ability to respond, in any situation. Your choices are as limited as your perceived picture allows. If you are determined to achieve your picture at all costs, you are limiting yourself to a response that will help keep the image you have or want to create. Even to the point of pretending or fooling yourself that things are not as they are and that what you really feel is only in your imagination. If you are pretending or fooling yourself you are doing so to others.

This is a major factor in so many relationships, families, partnerships and marriages breaking up. With the realisation that the picture is not as expected, you move on, often clinging to the picture, replacing the people and the things but not replacing the expectations or the picture itself. If you allow your belief system to remain, as it was when you were a child, being good, doing what's perceived as right, what everyone else is doing, so be it. You get what you want and you keep on getting it. When you choose to change and take actions you get a new experience. Your response to the changes that you are free to make, or not make, determines how you live in your picture or surroundings. The new experience must be yours – it must involve your feelings, your thoughts and your actions – not new surroundings, people or things.

The experience must come from within, not with or from somebody or something outside (which would be re – arranging, not changing). You must feel the changes. Your surroundings do not necessarily have to change. You have choice, free will. If you do not choose change, you are choosing things to remain as they are (so be it), hoping, wishing, even praying to an entity or deity outside of yourself for change. This too is choosing no change and comes from a belief system that you are not worthy, that you do not deserve the right to use your free will. Yet you will accept the will of an outside force such as luck, faith, destiny and divine intervention – all of which are created within the self – you create your own luck, hold your own faith or belief and choose your own destiny. You have free will – this is divine intervention. It is yours already. Meditation is a withdrawal from the conflicts of the outside world or forces, into the quietness and stillness. It is a way to show or say to yourself that you are loved. You love yourself enough to take the time and create a space to think, feel and act in a loving way towards yourself. Meditation need not involve ritual, though ritual can focus the mind and intentions. Practising meditation is one way to heal the hurt of the inner – child.

When you have found your inner – peace, you can then invite in your inner – child. By consciously remembering your feelings, thoughts and actions, you can look at issues from the perception of both the child and adult in you. This is where, when and how to change. Enter into this place, space or state with the intentions of changing the way you react when you leave and return to the conflicts and turmoil of the outer world. Start by looking at your repetitive emotional pattern; the feeling that keeps coming back. Sometimes it comes with a shrinking or lost and helpless, alone and rejected feeling. Remember the last time you felt like this. Do not get caught up in the reasons and circumstances. These have been changing throughout your life. The feelings have remained the same. Remember the moment of change, when the inner – child emerged and as you remember, sense the energy in and around you. Become aware of the energy. How it feels. How you feel just before it jumps you and takes over. For those who feel the need to, this is also a good place and time to trace back to where the feelings started. Understand it from the child's perception and explain to the child, as an adult you no longer need to feel hurt, unloved or fearful. Reassure, nurture and love the child. You may get flashbacks or unlock forgotten or buried memories or experiences. If you do not, don't go searching. It will happen when you are ready for it, if you need it to. Now look at your response to that feeling as an adult. When you recognise and understand the energy of the inner – child and how it takes over or jumps you, you can take back control. Say "stop!" It's ok, you no longer need to feel unloved.

This is where, when and how you can change your behaviour pattern; the way you act when the child energy takes over. You need to re – programme what your reaction will be when you next meet a situation that triggers your inner – child. React or act in a positive way. If you recognise what is happening, smile, rejoice and withdraw from conflict. Do something uplifting for yourself. Focus on the positive thought, feeling and action. If you can do this once, you can do it again. Then you have the ability to heal your inner – child and change how you feel and react to any situation you may find yourself in.

PICTURE LIFESTYLES

I can see through your successful front
I can see into your pain
I see that you are playing your part
A child in a grown ups' game.

I can see that you are working
From a picture in your mind
A picture painted, long ago
Never left behind.

I see you gather all your wants
And "must have's", to compare
With other people playing the game
Picture lifestyles everywhere
As you look around wanting bigger wants than theirs.

I can see through picture lifestyles
Into the sadness they emit
As a player gets frustrated
When a want they chose won't fit
Neatly, into the space in the picture of their mind
To act a part that they perceived
In pictures painted as a child.

It's not supposed to be like this
Tempers, sulks and atmospheres
So you just rearrange your picture
In your mind, but not out here.

I can see the disappointment
A missing sparkle from your eye
As you notice empty spaces
In the picture in your mind.

The silences
The hurtful looks
Weary as you tow the line
In someone else's picture
In someone else's mind.

CHAPTER TWELVE

HEALING

There are many forms of healing available and many levels we need healing on, not just the physical and there are many healers to choose from. Healers of the mind, healers of the body, healers of the spirit, new age/ alternative healers, conventional medicine and ancient medicine. There is a healer available at whatever time and at whatever level you seek it. There is also a healer in you. We are all healers. Self – healing is a process that starts with a thought about yourself, a feeling for yourself and most importantly, taking action for yourself. This may be in the form of simply going to a general practitioner for a check – up. This may lead to a surgeon, a herbalist for an allergy cure, a psychic for a reading, an aromatherapist for relaxation from stress, a shamanic healer for soul retrieval or a Reiki healing.

Whatever the reason or the healer, the key to self – healing is you taking the first step. This usually involves change or at least the will to change, at some level. It may be your routine, eating or exercise habits, addictions or changes to the way you react in certain circumstances. It could also involve changes to the way you perceive how things are or were. Whatever way it comes to you it will involve changing your reality. Your intention to change and your ability to change (this is free will) is healing in itself. Self – healing! Some forms of healing work only on one level. A physician or surgeon works on and in the body (the physical level), a psychiatrist or psychologist works on and in the mind (the mental level), a psychotherapist or councillor works with the emotional level. As multi – sensual and perceptual beings, we need to work to heal on every level that we are experiencing, not just the physical.

When you are ready, seek out a healing technique that works with all levels and then apply that healing. Your own energy field or aura is your most powerful tool in healing. All levels of being (including the human being) are contained within the aura. Healing through and with the aura can be practised by anybody without exception, just like meditation. All it needs is your willing participation.

Some simple yet powerful and effective methods include visualisation – just imagine – using your imagination has the power to create! This process starts from a thought in the mind, this in turn creates a possibility. Possibilities become reality (every possibility has the potential, though not all do). If the vision is held (where there is a will, there is a way) and energy added in the form of intentions and actions, an idea, vision, or thought can become a reality.

So it is with everything you can sense, see, smell, hear, feel and touch. It all started with and continues with, a thought, a vision in the mind. Our mind (see oneness and separation).

We are all one.

GROUNDING

It is important to be grounded in your reality. Grounding helps to keep us in the now. To face the issues we need to face up to (the ones we keep ignoring and wish they would just go away, but don't). It reinforces our connection with the earth, with life itself, with the bigger picture. It makes us feel worthwhile, useful, belonging, part of something more powerful than ourselves. Any type of healing needs to be grounded or anchored into existence (see exercise to ground).

WHITE LIGHT

White light breathing helps us to raise our energy levels or vibrations. It brings calm and a sense of rejuvenation to the physical and mental levels. On other levels it helps to loosen stuck energy in the form of negative thought forms (negative being not positive) or fear, allowing the issues to surface, to be acknowledged, owned and accepted as ours. This is taking responsibility. When negative thought forms leave, white light fills the void and heals. It also opens us up to the higher vibration of spirit, to do psychic or spiritual work, to receive and channel or transmit guidance and wisdom for ourselves and those who seek it (if they choose). Light workers work with this energy. It is also known as the breath of God, divine light or source.

Everything, all that is now and ever shall be, *is* the white light (see exercise for white light breathing).

CRYSTALS

The power of the earth or life itself is in the crystals. They contain wisdom far beyond our limited understanding. Healers throughout our existence on this planet and beyond have used them.

The membrane of every cell of every living thing is liquid crystal. This is what gives everything its' vibration. For everything has, including us, a vibration and an aura or energy field.

Crystals store information. Quartz, silicone and fibre – optics, just to name three, are widely used in the electronic, communication, aviation and medical industries. From your watch to your computer, your cell phone to the auto – pilot that can land a plane, from a blade of grass to a space probe - where would we be without them? Crystals are used in healing and work with our energy fields through our chakras, our energy points on, in and through our bodies.

There are seven major chakra points on the body, an eighth one is now being activated in all people (it is already active in some and all new - born children). Each point has it's own corresponding colour. Placing a crystal or stone of similar colour on, above or below the chakra point, helps balance us on every level. This brings us into harmony with our surroundings and how we exist in those surroundings. Flowers can also be used.

Crystals can also imbalance us in our surroundings, effecting our energy fields and levels, resulting in us feeling zapped, lethargic or spaced out. Grounding regularly and using a chakra set (the seven coloured stones/ crystals) brings us back to balance and good form.

EXERCISE TO GROUND

There are obvious ways to ground oneself. Walking, working or playing on the ground, connecting with the energy of the earth and feeling a connection. We all do these things all the time but we don't always feel connected.

Doing one of these simple exercises regularly will help you feel that connection. Even just for a few moments.

Close your eyes, sit or stand comfortably, planting your feet firmly on the ground or floor.

Take three or four long, slow, deep breaths. Hold for two or three seconds and slowly release.

Imagine roots growing out of your feet, down into the earth, deeper and deeper. Into level after level of soil and rock, anchoring onto and around big heavy boulders.

Now visualise the air that you are breathing flowing through your body, down through your feet into the ground. Down through the roots and deep into the earth.

Focus your attention onto nothing, a blank screen. Feel the energy.

Do this as often and for as long as you want to or need to.

That is it, you are grounded.

Another method is to visualise yourself standing on sand. Physically twist your feet from side to side and visualise your feet sinking into the sand. Even better, go to the beach! The aim is to focus your attention or consciousness to your connection with earth and it's energy.

Walking bare foot on grass is also very grounding. Wear red socks!

If you have a chakra set, place the red stone at your feet.

WHITE LIGHT BREATHING

Do some grounding before you start if this is new to you.

Looking into the flame of a candle for a few seconds may help you with this visualisation.

Sit in a comfortable and relaxed position.

Close your eyes and imagine that the air around you is made of bright, white light and that you can breathe this light into you.

Fill your lungs with the light, taking deep, slow breaths and allow the light to spill out from your lungs into your chest cavity.

With each "in breath", move the light down, through your legs and feet and into the ground.

Fill your shoulders and arms and allow the light to flow out of your hands and into your aura.

Breathe light into your throat, the back of your head, scalp, forehead, face and jaw, back into your throat and into your heart.

Allow the light to move out through your body, like the glow from a flame, filling your aura with light.

You can stay in this glow as often and for as long as you wish to. In fact, you can live your whole life in this warm peaceful state. For it is a state of enlightenment. Each time you do this exercise you are adding energy to your light or spirit body, the part of you that is eternal. You open up to your inner – knowing, the soul of the matter. This is a safe place or state of mind to meet your guides.

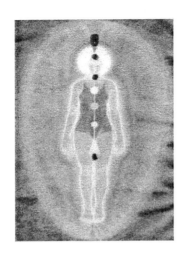 

AURA AND CHAKRA POINTS.   CHAKRA SET.

7th..........Crown chakra, clear crystal. Place the stone above the head.

6th..........Brow chakra, purple/ indigo. Place stone on the forehead.

5th..........Throat chakra, blue. Place stone on the throat.

4th..........Heart chakra, green or pink. Place stone on the centre of the chest.

3rd..........Solar plexus chakra, yellow. Place stone on the centre of the stomach.

2nd..........Sacral chakra, orange/ reddish. Place the stone on the lower stomach.

1st..........Base or root chakra, red. Place the stone above the knees.

The stones do not have to be shop bought or semi – precious. Any natural stone of similar colour plus your intention to use it as a healing tool will do.

Create a relaxing atmosphere (candles, incense, soft music). Lay down and position the stones.

Count as you breathe. Try to visualise the numbers, one in, one out, two in, two out, three in, three out and so on.

See the numbers coming as you breathe in and going as you breathe out.

If you reach a hundred, start again. Don't try too hard. If your mind drifts, go with it. If you are not relaxed, try later, but keep on trying – it will work.

INNER SPACE

Behind the doorways of your eyes,
lies a different realm.
When you close the doors to the outside,
you open the doors to within.

You see colour and shape in your minds' eye.
A third one that sees,
In this place called infinity,
Inner space.

Through this door you can travel in spirit,
to the past and what is to come.
To the dream world we enter so often,
forgetting our journey has already begun.

Your insight can play you a memory at will.
Like a movie or maybe a snapshot, quite still.
A flashback keeps coming and will do, until
you find knowledge, lessons and meaning,
to use for your ongoing healing.

Intention is what you begin with
and direction - which way, up or down?
The upper world of the angels and saints,
spiritual teachers and guides,

temples and god beyond the clouds.
Feelings of love and peace will come back from this place
and you can keep them inside.

The lower world of spirit once earth – bound,
the land, the sea, the air.
Animals, sea creatures and birds wait to meet you there,
you can fly, you can swim,
go running with them,
they give you a great sense of belonging within.

They warn you of wrong turns or slips off your path
and show you the right one for you to be on,
and protect you as you journey.
In both worlds you can ask questions,
for guidance for you, for somebody else.
Meet your loved - ones who have travelled before you,
once more,
you will see that you are spirit yourself.

When you open the doorway of your eyes once again,
into the material realm,
question yourself on your chosen path,
listen for guidance,
It will come from within,
the universe that you are a part of.
This place.
The universe, is part of your inner space.

CHAPTER THIRTEEN

MESSAGES FROM SPIRIT

These messages are written as they were given to me, without any editing.

MESSAGE TO HUMAN – KIND

You know nothing of the world you occupy.
You have not seen the world you live in.
Look and feel.
You try too hard to understand.
That understanding is not for your world or your existence in it.
You rely on your own limited view – point.
Your so – called experts will always only know within limited knowledge.
The power of the sea and water are your life force.
Use the energy contained there.
You are destroying what you need to survive.
You are not open to anything outside of your own limited knowledge being possible.
Your knowledge is limited.
Possibilities are open - ended.
You call this infinity.
Open up your mind to the power.

We use the word power, not as you do, but as a descriptive
word for the energy you need to survive.
Open your eyes to the power that is all encompassing.
You have the knowledge to harness and distribute this.
You have no need and it is not necessary for you to create
your own power, for you do not understand the delicate
nature of the planet you live on.
You seek other worlds.
These will come, in time.
Your time.
Open up your mind.
Know the difference between knowing and knowledge.
Feel your faith.
For faith is feeling and living, not heard and believed.
There is more than one explanation, more than one
possibility.
To the Red Army:
The power is universal.
It does not belong to any one group of beings.
Your weapons of destruction are the limited knowledge
you possess.
Their destructive power is open – ended.
Listen to your inner – self.
Hear your future lives, crying to be lived.

To humanity you are not a race, you are not in a race.
Slow down, feel.
Slow down.
Listen to the birds.
Feel the energy.

KARMA

Karma......The balance of light and not – light. This has been interpreted as good over bad, right over wrong - opposing forces. There are no opposing forces. All energy flows as one. Light and not – light are one.

I am deliberately not using the words darkness and evil because of the perception the collective consciousness has created around these words. There are no demons and devils. No dark forces at work. No hell. No evil one, except for the ones you create for yourselves.

The same is true for the light. For some, there are no spirit world, angels, no eternity and no heaven, no God, until it is brought into creation in the self.
There is no right or wrong, good or bad. There is no one judging you - no punishment and no judgement day. There is no death. There is only light and not – light.

Light is love, pure unconditional love.

Not – light is the absence of love.

This is the simple truth.

The planet revolves or rotates in a balanced atmosphere of light and not light. Light is not sunlight, yet it does come from the sun, as well as the entire universe. The earth sends light into the universe.

Not – light is not the absence of sunlight nor is it darkness. It is simply the absence of love or light. Not – light or the absence of love, creates fear in people, you, all of you. All fear is the absence of love, unconditional love of yourself.

All human conditions are based on this principal or spiritual law. Love is reaching out, to touch, to experience life in the moment - in the ever changing now. Fear will stop this. Fear will keep you trapped in what's called the past or what you perceive as the future. This is a normal human condition. All, who incarnate into the human or earth experience, will experience fear (some have interpreted this as original sin). No ritual can cleanse or wash away fear. Without fear, we would not recognise its' absence, which is love. Fear is part of the earth experience, of all human existence.
Earth offers the incarnating spirit endless opportunities to face or recognise the fear and transmute or replace it with love or light. Understanding this with the mind is not enough to transmute fear, although it is the first step in the process. The transmutation, changing and replacing must be experienced in your heart – centre, not your physical heart but your heart centre - the seat of your soul, the centre of your being.

This is karma. How much fear you replaced during an incarnation or lifetime. How much you became enlightened. Looking for details about past life or after –

death karma is not experiencing the now. The ever changing now is the only place to balance karma.

Fear (not light) and light are creative forces or powers. They bring into reality what humanity as a whole (the collective, one being) and humans individually create through their thoughts, words and actions. They are your servants. No questions asked, no cautions, no warnings and no judgement. They are your tools. They mould themselves to suit your reality in the ever changing now.

Light and not light are/ is the ever changing now. You choose how you want to experience now. The forces change the moment you choose. Fear manifests in many, many ways. In fact, it adjusts to suit the individual and individuals make up the collective. When the individual chooses change from the heart – centre, changes occur in their life circumstances and also how they react to these changes. When enough individuals choose change from their heart – centres, changes occur in the circumstances that effect the collective. The collective can only change as individuals change themselves.

The changes people have to make are known by names such as challenges, obstacles, blocks, lessons, missions, life purpose and many more. Indeed, this is what they are. The way in which you face them creates the circumstances and conditions you live in.

Many spirits who incarnate do not face their fears. This is not failure. There are no limits, rules or boundaries. Only experiences which bring the opportunity to face your fear. When you choose change voluntarily it makes the fear less frightening than when change is forced onto you due to the changes made by another or others. Either way, the fear will be faced and opportunities will be presented to you time and time again, lifetime after lifetime until you choose love over fear. Now is the only time you can do this. Now is the only time there is. When you do not want to experience something any more or due to the actions of a collective, you will face the fear of change.

LIGHTEN UP

Don't be afraid of the darkness,
don't invite in panic and fright.
Keep them out by knowing,
you have an internal light.

Imagine your heart as a battery,
pumping white light through your veins.
Recharging itself from the earth, through your feet,
from the universe, through your crown to your brain.

Harness this energy flow.
Insulate yourself in an invisible shell,
protecting you in its glow.
Lifting your burdens,
help keeping you well.

Breathe this light into your lungs.
Allow the light to spill out,
down your legs and your arms,
out your fingers and toes.
Fill up your head as you breathe light in through your nose.

Imagine then, as you breathe out,
negative clouds being expelled through your mouth.
Colour these clouds dark, black or grey.
Light penetrates darkness, it must go away.

Label or name these clouds,
with the feelings you would like to clear.
Worry and stress,
untangle the mess,
emptiness, doubt, stubbornness, fear.

Concentrate on positive thinking,
Introduce yourself to your soul.
Together, plan a direction,
a dream, destination, a challenge and a goal.

Take time to yourself because you're worth it.
Be you child, woman or man.
Love yourself first, then love others.
Enjoy life as much as you can.
It's a journey.
A part of a whole bigger plan.

WHAT LOVE IS

Love is an essence. A very fine vibration not unlike tiny dust particles that you cannot see until they settle or get caught in a shaft of light. Except love has no form therefore any shape or weight. It has colour yet it cannot be seen. It is like radio signals, microwaves and thoughts. It can be touched and it can touch. You either have it or you crave for it. You either see it everywhere or you search for it everywhere. You recognise its vibrations when you come into contact with it or you recognise its absence.

It is in the air you breathe, the food you eat and the water you drink. Every cell and atom, every particle of DNA contains this essence. There is no half – way. You feel love or you don't. Lip service, using the word love, is not love. When you feel love you are love. It permeates your being and over – flows from you onto others.

It exists only in the moment. With love, you exist in the moment. The moment is now, always now. Without love you have removed yourself from the moment. Love is not happiness. It creates the conditions for happiness to thrive. Happiness without love is an illusion, believing love is a feeling that comes with and from something outside of you - from parents, family, lovers, partners, children, houses, money, cars and sex. Behind the illusion lies disappointments. Behind the disappointments lies truth.

174

Truth is love. Look beyond the illusion, beyond the disappointments for the truth of your reality. It is then that you are aware of love. When people say they "make" love, what they are experiencing is the exclusion of all other thoughts and feelings leaving only love and the moment.

I AM THAT I AM

When you feel bitter you are in the dark. When colours affect you in a negative way you are also in the dark. The dark forces (the ones we create ourselves) are using you if another persons' skin colour effects you or the colour of the flag of another country.

It has been said many times in the past and it has to be said many times in the future. It will be said by *all* people of *all* colours, in every country of the planet. The words will be chanted. The world will chant together in unison - Across time – zones and continents, oceans and seas. It will be chanted in homes and in the open, out loud and in silence. The words are *"I am that I am"*.

There shall be no need for any other affirmation except I am that I am, in the now. When all your thoughts and energies are taken from the past and the future and focused into the now, you are truly alive and on your way back to light. The source of light itself. The challenges you face are on a day to day, hour to hour, moment to moment basis. When you have finally stopped this in your own mind and heart, you will have found me for *"I am"* the light, the source, the source of light.

WORLD TRADE CENTRE

All is well.

I am the pilot of the plane.

I am the passenger.

I am in the building.

I am on the street below.

I am creating your will.

Your will is my will, you, all of you, can create in me, with me, through me, a peaceful world by simply, yet meaningfully saying "I (say your own name), live in a peaceful world. I am that I am, I am that I am".

America is experiencing the law of return. What you give to another also you will receive unto you.

World war. World peace. I am creating your will. What is your will?

Authors note: I had a vision of the events two years previous to September 11th. This message is the response I received when I asked source, as I watched the actual events unfolding, why?

THE MOMENT OF ENLIGHTENMENT

I have seen many wonderful things in my life until this moment but never have I seen how much all the wonderful things depend on me being wonderful too. It is interdependency. Nothing can exist on its own yet nothing can exist until it is truly free and on its own.

In spirit, we exist on our own yet we are part of the one, the divine, the God - head or source. It has many names. We are all part of the one as you are, on earth. You must find your oneness with your God – head. It is an individual journey all have to make as one, yet alone. Use all your senses.

Your instincts are your most vital tool. Use them for yourself. Allow others to use their own. Involve others on your journey for they will learn from you and you from them.

Time is a barrier you have broken when you live in the now and exist in the now. The now is the moment and space you occupy. The place you return to when you stop reliving past feelings and emotions. Where you are when you are not away ahead of yourself into the future - rearranging what is not in your reality.

The now is the life of interaction where changes are made. New experiences are experienced here, lessons learnt from old ones and new ones invited in. Goals and dreams are created here and manifested into your reality. When you set yourself a goal or dream, you trigger off a chain of events inter – linked with the energy of your creator. You are one with this energy, helping to create your own reality. No matter what your present circumstances are, you have the ability to create new ones, individually and so collectively.

GRATITUDE

What we are healing is ourselves - our past, our present and our future.

One at a time we are born. One at a time we shall heal.

Do not strive for perfection, your perfect moment is always now.

Accept it as it is with gratitude. Live in gratitude.

Return to gratitude when you notice its' absence.

I CHANGED

I'd love things to change, but they wont.
I wish things would change, but they don't.
I dream and I pray
for change every day.
I hope I'm not hoping against hope.

I look out my window and wait,
for change to arrive at my gate.
To darken my door,
be entertained on the floor.
I wait
and I wait
and I wait.

Sitting waiting around is a chore.
Looking out my front window's a bore.
Getting older not younger,
getting weaker not stronger
and I'd love to live life a bit more.

No change yesterday.
No change today.
No change tomorrow.
It will always be that way.
These are the dark thoughts misting my mind.
If the no was not there I think I'd be fine.

Then I realised one day,

what's keeping no there.
It's me,
It's my pride,
my shyness,
my fear.
Negative thoughts from the mists of my mind,
blocking my way,
like a cage I'm behind
and I'm holding the bars,
looking outward with envy,
self-doubt,
self-pity.
And sometimes I get angry.

One day the sun,
shining down on my face,
lifted the mist of my mind.
A positive thought took negative space,
I opened my windows and doors.
The perfection of birdsong,
drifted into my ear.
Lifting my spirits,
releasing my fear.

A fresh breeze made me shiver for a moment or two.
It shook off my pride and my envy.
Another breeze came and blew them away.
They won't block me anymore.
So without them now, I've no need to get angry.
It's just me and my doubts,
between me and the door.

I won't, I don't and I can't.
I couldn't, shouldn't or shan't.
Negative words get in the way.
What will people think?
What will people say?
Will I feel like a fool, if I fail something I try?
Are they pointing at me? O god I could die!
I'm feeling so helpless and I want to know why?

I crumple down into a ball on the floor.
A handful of paces,
that's all that the space is.
Then my doubt makes me think, do I want change at all?
Just a few feet away, but I'm not going to crawl.

Then some new feelings came from inside.
Filling the void left behind by my blown away pride.
My self-love and free will, they swelled up and I cried,
tears of rejoicing, for I thought they had died.
As I picked myself up,
I felt a new sense of meaning.
Something had started,
I call it self-healing.

Now I no longer sit around and wait.
Change came from within me, not in through my front
gate.
I stand on my doorstep, my threshold to life.
The world's at my feet, I can do what I like.

I don't wish for or dream of,

for change I don't pray.
I made the difference,
something different each day.
It can be small, like a walk,
a thought or a talk.
I take in a movie or a play
or brave new interests.
A hobby,
new work,
ambitions to travel abound.
New places,
new smells,
new people,
new sounds.

Now I live to love life.
It's mine and I'm right.
When I started being different,
It felt a bit strange.
But now I'll try anything,
just for a change.

ISBN 141200415-2